DEPARTMENT OF HEALTH

Taking Research Seriously

Means of improving and assessing the use and dissemination of research

Ann Richardson
Christine Jackson
Wendy Sykes

Social and Community Planning Research

LONDON: HMSO

Contents

Foreword

In 1988, the Research Management Division of what was then the Department of Health and Social Security asked Ann Richardson to look at how better use might be made of the research commissioned for the Department. We were conscious that valuable research was being produced through Departmental funding and the results were not sufficiently widely known about or used. At the same time, we wanted to consider whether it was possible to evaluate the usefulness of the studies commissioned by the Division.

Dr Richardson and her colleagues have addressed the issues in a very thorough and helpful way and their resulting report covers a lot of important territory. They have identified thought-provoking possibilities for improving the dissemination and use of research and have clarified some of the complex issues regarding assessment. In the Deparment of Health we shall regard Dr Richardson's report as a source document as we consider how to disseminate research more effectively and how to monitor performance in this respect. The report is also available to colleagues in the Department of Social Security.

The issues covered in the report are salient beyond our own Department. We are not alone in needing to look at ways of improving and assessing research dissemination and use. Except for a few matters of detail, the report should be of interest to all funding agencies.

We are therefore very pleased to make this work available to a much wider audience through its publication by HMSO. We hope that it will stimulate discussion and debate.

J H Barnes
Director of Research Management
Department of Health

April 1989

Executive Summary

Aims and methods

This exercise was commissioned by the Department of Health and Social Security to consider:

- means of improving the use and dissemination of research
- means of assessing the use and dissemination of research.

Discussions were held with customers and research managers in the DH/DSS, local users of research and researchers themselves.

Principal Recommendations

Research use should be widely interpreted to include increased understanding and illumination as well as direct use for policy. Although much research is well disseminated and well used, there is substantial room for improvement.

Research Management Division *should:*

- develop a strategic approach to research dissemination and use
- build attention to dissemination into the job description of liaison officers
- include a dissemination period in research contracts
- provide resources for dissemination
- advise customers on research which may be useful
- assess researchers on their dissemination efforts
- establish a dissemination database

Policy Divisions *should:*

- commission research which is likely to be useful
- specify clearly the aims of individual studies
- clarify the products wanted from each study
- take an active interest in the research sponsored
- help to disseminate research findings
- consider the employment of specialist staff to advise on research
- commission focussed reviews of existing research

Researchers *should:*

- take principal responsibility for dissemination
- write time for dissemination into research plans and proposals
- complete specified reports or other publications on time
- ensure that publications are clearly targeted to specific audiences
- prepare attractive and accessible material
- produce and distribute summaries of their research
- disseminate their research imaginatively and widely

Overall, there is a need for a clear *commitment* to research, with resources provided for its dissemination and responsibility taken for its use.

Preface

P.1 What can be done to ensure that the best possible use is made of the findings of research? How can the value of individual projects and programmes be assessed? This report was commissioned by the then Department of Health and Social Security (DHSS) to address these important questions. Its immediate genesis was a concern to develop some measures of research utility, in response to pressures to justify expenditure in this area along with other government activity. At the same time, it was felt that some attention to improving research dissemination and use would be beneficial. An independent enquiry in this broad area seemed appropriate.

P.2 This study was carried out by three researchers, but was not in essence a typical research project. Our aim was not to collect data about research use and dissemination but ideas about problems and possible solutions. We talked to a wide range of people – research users, research managers and researchers themselves – about the issues under question. Occasionally, contrary to normal interviewing practice, we took issue with our respondents, pushing ideas to see where they would go. At all times, our aim was to hone an argument or set of arguments – not to count those in any one corner. As with other qualitative research of this kind, no claim can be made that the discussions covered a representative sample. But they did elicit a wealth of ideas about problems and sources of improvement. A short note on our research methods, including the range of people interviewed, is provided in Annex 3.

P.3 We must stress that this was essentially a modest exercise, undertaken within a short time span. We could not – and did not try to – cover all subject areas encompassed by what became early on in our work the two Departments of Health and Social Security (referred to here as the DH/DSS). The latter in particular received much less attention, as the bulk of DHSS research fell within the remit of what became the DH. In addition, in preparing this report, we have had to stick fairly closely to the issues at hand. We have not set the issues in a philosophical or historical context. Nor have we systematically reviewed the burgeoning literature on the subject, although we have drawn on this as appropriate. By pulling together the ideas of those we spoke to and adding some of our own, our principal aim has been to produce a potentially *useful* document.

P.4 This study took place during a period of considerable political turmoil in the research world. General pressure on higher education meant that academics had both a lot on their minds and a lot to say. In particular, they were aware of the hard financial implications of exercises such as that carried out by the then University Grants Committee (UGC) to assess the research performance of academic departments. The Economic and Social Research Council (ESRC) was also in the process of considering some similar issues. While we expected these activities might complicate our endeavours, because of a beleaguered feeling among researchers, in fact they probably made it easier as a lot of thinking was going on. Indeed, we found considerable enthusiasm for our exercise and emerged with a high level of optimism about the potential for change.

P.5 This report is concerned to clarify and make recommendations on issues surrounding both the *improvement* and the *assessment* of research dissemination and use. It reflects our view that these are very distinct matters. In principle as well as practice, it is possible to improve without assessing and to assess without improving (although the two are frequently interlinked). Therefore, following a discussion of some general issues (chapter 1), the report is divided into a discussion of improving dissemination (chapter 2) and use (chapter 3) and a discussion of assessing these activities (chapter 4). The concluding chapter calls attention to some broader issues raised by the study. Our general argument and principal recommendations are set out in summary form at the outset and a one page 'executive summary' is also provided.

P.6 As always, we must acknowledge the immense help we have been given throughout the course of this exercise. We are especially grateful to Hazel Canter, who eased our path in a variety of ways. A Steering Group, chaired by the Deputy Chief Scientist, Dr Jeremy Metters, provided much useful guidance and support. From Social and Community Planning Research, Jill Keegan provided enormous help with the interviewing and Jane Ritchie served as a valuable sounding board as the occasion arose. A brief word of thanks (or apology) is due to Professor Ronald Dworkin, whose title *Taking Rights Seriously* we have borrowed here. A number of people kindly read and commented on the final draft, including Professor Walter Holland, Professor Geoffrey Oldham and Dr Christopher Pollitt. Finally, we are very grateful indeed to the many people around the country who gave us their time and thoughts on the issues.

Summary of Argument and Recommendations

S.1 The concept of research use needs to be broadly defined, to include indirect and long-term changes in the ways issues are discussed as well as immediate use by policy-makers. It includes gaining information, clarification and illumination as well as translating research directly into policy or practice (paras 1.11 – 1.17).

S.2 There are many different users of research (paras 1.18 – 1.22); this study addresses the needs of public agencies, both the direct customers and local policy-makers and practitioners (para 1.39).

S.3 Much research is well disseminated to many differing audiences (paras 2.3 – 2.14) and well used in differing ways (paras 3.3 – 3.10). But there are also problems. Research is often not fully disseminated for a wide range of professional and practical reasons (paras 2.16 – 2.26). It is often not fully used because of political as well as practical considerations (paras 3.11 – 3.26).

S.4 While some of these problems are not amenable to change, many steps can be suggested to improve both dissemination and use.

Recommendations for Research Management Division*

Improving research dissemination

S.5 RMD needs to establish a strategic approach to dissemination, giving legitimacy to such activity and building in attention to dissemination at all stages of research management (paras 2.27 – 2.28).

S.6 RMD should provide the resources and other forms of support to enable researchers to carry out dissemination; dissemination time specified in proposals should be welcomed and should not prejudice the chances of the applicant. Principal responsibility for dissemination should be assigned to researchers; RMD should commend them for their dissemination efforts (paras 2.29 – 31).

S.7 All liaison officers should have some responsibility for advising on and encouraging dissemination activities. While there should not be a separate dissemination unit, some expertise in routine aspects of dissemination should be developed among clerical or junior administrative staff (paras 5.40 – 5.43).

S.8 More advice should be given to researchers on dissemination; RMD should consider the preparation of guidelines, the provision of training and practical help (para 2.33).

---

* At the time of writing, RMD had just been split between the Departments of Health and Social Security. Only the Department of Health retained the name. We use this term generically to refer to those carrying out research management functions.

S.9 RMD should help researchers to think about the appropriate amount and kinds of dissemination, both written and oral (para 2.34). Some written material is essential, but the preparation of a special research report for the Department(s) should be actively discouraged, unless the commissioning customer is the primary audience and wants such a report; a technical report on methods should always be available (paras 2.81 – 2.82).

S.10 The expected products of a study should be specified in the research contract and reviewed during the course of the project with customers and researchers (paras 2.36 – 2.37). RMD should reassure researchers that their ability to publish findings will not be withheld unreasonably; any material not intended for publication should be clarified at the outset (para 2.38).

S.11 Researchers should be assessed in part on their dissemination efforts, through the refereeing system and the Chief Scientist's Visit, in order to increase attention to such activity (paras 4.56 – 4.57).

S.12 More resources should be available for dissemination. A dissemination phase should be funded at the end of projects; alternatively, a set proportion of the time and resources in a contract should be able to be used to disseminate earlier work. Researchers might be provided with a financial incentive for producing readable material, possibly equivalent to the costs of hiring someone else to do so (paras 2.41 – 2.49).

S.13 RMD should have a budget explicitly designated for dissemination activities, which should be widely publicised. This should be available for disseminating research initially funded not only by RMD but also by other funding agencies (paras 2.50 – 2.51).

S.14 Consideration should be given to funding research tranlators, who might revise researchers' material for selected audiences or disseminate it in other ways (paras 2.53 – 2.64).

S.15 More vehicles for publicising research to potential users should be considered. These might include a new journal or additional abstracting services. The availability of the latter, particularly on-line, should be well publicised to researchers and all potential users (paras 2.65 – 2.68).

S.16 The annual R&D Handbook should be better publicised and reorganised. Reports should be more widely publicised to customers and researchers (paras 2.69 – 2.70).

Improving research use

S.17 RMD should establish that the usefulness of research – widely interpreted – is an important criterion in its funding. It should set up a strategy on research use. More help should be provided to customers in thinking through the usefulness of research commissioned (paras 3.35 – 3.38).

S.18 Customers and researchers should be encouraged to work together on the design of projects and to maintain contact throughout the course of a study. This does not mean direction by customers (paras 3.35 – 3.58).

S.19 Customers' attention should be drawn to research beyond that directly commissioned (paras 3.59 – 3.60).

S.20 RMD should set up internal seminars for customers on how to use research; existing seminars on research findings should be better publicised (paras 3.43 and 3.63).

S.21 RMD should help customers to understand the limits of research as well as its potential contribution. Consideration should be given to the preparation of a 'users manual' on research for customers (paras 3.36 – 3.42).

S.22. Attention should be given to means of publicising research to local policy-makers and practitioners (paras 3.70 and 3.79).

S.23 To increase the funding of research of interest to local users, research advisory groups involving local spokesmen should be established to discuss research priorities in specific fields. Those involved might include practitioners, such as medical specialists, as well as officers or managers with a policy brief, depending on the subject (paras 3.67 – 3.69).

S.24 Comments on the usefulness of research should be explicitly solicited from referees at the proposal stage, as well as when projects are completed (paras 4.56 – 4.57). Prior dissemination efforts should be taken into account when considering future funding (para 2.30).

Assessing research dissemination and use

S.25 We assume that the purposes of an assessment exercise are: i) to help determine appropriate expenditure on research, by assessing whether research is useful or used; ii) to assist decisions on future funding, by distinguishing those researchers who produce useful or used research; and iii) to improve the use of research by identifying problem areas in research use, management and the process of research (paras 4.3 – 4.14).

S.26 While no one of these purposes is easily achieved, current practice could be improved (paras 4.15 – 4.18).

S.27 A dissemination database should be set up, to document all formal dissemination activities undertaken by units, programmes and individual researchers. This would include all publications and papers given to conferences and seminars as well as consultancy and development work. Attention should be given to how such information might be used, including problems around the interpretation of the data. This is essentially an extension of current systems for documenting publications arising from projects (paras 4.19 – 4.37).

S.28 Studies of the ways in which research is used should be funded to learn more about how people find out about research, how they use it and what can be done to increase such use. These studies might involve quantitative and qualitative methods; case studies of individual programmes may be particularly useful (paras 4.38 – 4.54).

S.29 Existing assessment procedures should be reviewed to ensure full attention to questions of the dissemination and use of research (paras 4.45 – 4.46).

S.30 Current review procedures for researchers should give more explicit attention to dissemination, both when individual studies are refereed and, in the case of units, at the time of the Chief Scientist's visit. Self-assessment systems should be given consideration, perhaps built into the research contract (paras 4.56 – 4.63).

S.31 The introduction of citation analysis is not recommended, as it does not measure the kind of use of interest to the DH/DSS (paras 4.64 – 4.70).

S.32 Any assessment systems introduced should be regularly reviewed (para 4.74). They should be discussed widely with those affected – customers, research management and researchers themselves – before being implemented (para 4.35). A consultation phase for this exercise would provide one vehicle for such discussion (paras 5.74 – 5.75).

General issues affecting RMD

S.33 Liaison officers should establish a 'service' orientation to customers, seeking to provide or facilitate whatever research services they most want. They should see themselves as responsible for raising the status of research among customers (paras 5.47 – 5.49).

S.34 The role of liaison officers with respect to researchers should be clarified. They should seek to be more open, explaining the reasons for decisions. Liaison officers should feed information back to researchers about the use of their research (paras 3.93 and 5.50 – 5.51).

S.35 Liaison officers should be encouraged to be practising researchers part-time, perhaps initially on a trial basis; this might help them to become more fully familiar with their field of expertise (paras 5.54 – 5.55).

S.36 Internal workshops should be arranged for liaison officers to exchange ideas on research management practice. Means of increasing interaction with people in similar jobs in other departments and elsewhere should also be considered (paras 5.56 – 5.57).

S.37 The in-service training of liaison officers may need attention, to create clearer systems of operating, encourage a service-oriented approach and improve where necessary their research expertise (para 5.58).

Recommendations for policy divisions

Improving research dissemination

S.38 Customers should take a more active role with respect to dissemination, advising researchers where appropriate (para 2.32).

S.39 Customers should discuss the expected products from a study with RMD and researchers. They should clarify whether they feel the production of a special research report is necessary. They may more appropriately encourage researchers to give them publications prepared for other purposes (paras 2.81 – 2.82).

S.40 Advice on the distribution of research summaries should be given by customers as well as help in disseminating them (para 2.80).

Improving research use

S.41 A strategic look should be given to long and short-term research needs; customers should fund research which is likely to be useful (paras 3.29 – 3.33).

S.42 Customers should take an active role at the outset of a study and throughout its course, discussing both the expected products and how they will be used with researchers (paras 3.35 – 3.58).

S.43 The expected use of a study should be specified in writing as well as the kind of products expected and for whom they would be prepared (para 3.39).

S.44 Customers should expect to give research reports (or other publications) considerable attention; if these are passed to junior staff to read, customers should ensure that they understand their contents (para 3.56). They should invite researchers to discuss their findings in informal meetings after the completion of the report or other publications (para 3.57).

S.45 Consideration should be given to the employment of research specialists to advise on research, translate findings and write overview briefing papers (paras 3.60 – 3.61).

S.46 Literature surveys and overviews should be commissioned as appropriate, to help customers learn about particular fields (para 3.62). Customers should ensure that they have adequate arrangements for knowing what research has already been commissioned (para 3.64).

S.47 Attention should be given to means of publicising relevant research to local policy-makers and practitioners (paras 3.70 – 3.79).

S.48 Researchers should be invited in to discuss issues as they arise, drawing on their expertise beyond the specific products of their research (paras 3.81 – 3.86).

Recommendations for the DH/DSS (general)

S.49 There is a broad need for commitment to research, not simply in terms of providing resources but in taking responsibility for findings and putting them into practice (paras 5.80 – 5.86).

S.50 The underlying aims of funded research should be clarified, that is whether it is commissioned for its contribution to 'enlightenment', to help with specific decisions or both. Attention also needs to be given to the audiences appropriately targeted; a broad interpretation, including attention to local research needs, is recommended (paras 5.2 – 5.11).

S.51 In determining research priorities, the system of priority themes may need to be reviewed in a few years' time to assess whether it is working well. Some flexibility should be assured in the system. There is strong concern for more research on the delivery of health and social services. There is also interest in more development work and focussed literature surveys (paras 5.20 – 5.28).

S.52 Funding for research should not be reduced and, if possible, increased. Funding to enable more researchers to be employed on a more stable basis (for more than the duration of one project) should be increased. Greater stability might improve research use, as it would help researchers to develop greater expertise in a given field and to invest in relationships with relevant customers (and vice versa) (paras 5.62 – 5.65).

S.53 Funding of research which may have no specific or immediate use should be primarily but not exclusively the responsibility of research councils. Funding of research of practical use should also be partly but not exclusively the domain of local or health authorities (paras 5.66 – 5.71). Systems should be established to ensure that local priorities are reflected in the commissioning process (paras 3.68 – 3.69).

S.54 A dissemination/consultation phase should be set up for this exercise, to enable researchers, research managers and research users to comment on issues raised in this report. More research should be undertaken on research use, especially at local level; an inquiry on development work would also be valuable (paras 5.73 – 5.75).

Recommendations for researchers

Improving research dissemination

S.55 Researchers should assume that they have principal responsibility for dissemination and ensure that their results are accessible to the widest possible audience (paras 2.28 – 2.30.).

S.56 Researchers should write dissemination into their initial proposals; they should ask for the specification of clear products in their research contract, with a sufficient budget to carry out such work. This specification should be reviewed during the course of a study with research managers and customers; researchers should call attention to any new audiences or dissemination activities identified (paras 2.36 – 2.37).

S.57 Careful attention should be given to the amount and nature of dissemination activities. Consideration should be given to more publications in trade journals, popular magazines and the journals of voluntary organisations (paras 2.73 – 2.78).

S.58 Research summaries should be produced, setting out the conclusions and recommendations. These should be widely distributed to different audiences (paras 2.79 – 2.80 and 3.73).

S.59 Researchers should seek to give papers to conferences and workshops involving a wide range of audiences; they should also undertake development work where appropriate (paras 2.83 – 2.87). They should also explore other means of publicising their results, for instance through radio and television and the production of videos and cassette tapes (paras 2.88 – 2.90).

Improving research use

S.60 Attention should be given to the potential use of the products of research from the outset. These should be produced on time. Researchers should seek to meet customers' needs in material prepared for them. Attention should be paid to making research findings salient to and understandable by those who will read them (paras 3.49 – 3.53 and 3.71 – 3.72).

S.61 Researchers should seek active involvement with customers, as well as RMD, at the outset of a study and throughout its course (paras 3.35 – 3.58).

S.62 Reports for customers or other publications should be concise and include a summary. Researchers should be selective in the presentation of their data. A technical report on methods should always be available (paras 3.51 – 3.53).

S.63 All publications should feel accessible and be attractively presented (para 3.72).

S.64 Researchers should seek active involvement at local level, marketing their results where relevant (paras 3.70 – 3.74 and 3.79).

NB   A summary in a different form is provided in Annex 2, where a number of recommendations are pulled together in a description of good research practice.

CHAPTER 1

Introducing the Issues

1.1 Many trees have been felled in the interest of exploring the relationship between research and policy. We see no reason to add to their number. But we cannot sensibly explore how to improve or assess the use of research without first examining some underlying issues, such as what is *meant* by research use. Similarly, there is a need to consider different kinds of research and the different audiences to which research may be addressed. In this short chapter we undertake a brief ground-clearing exercise on these issues; at the end, we summarise what we have assumed to be the key concerns of the DH/DSS here.

Why study use?

1.2 It is important to begin by raising one question underlying our whole study – why consider use? Is it appropriate to look for means of assessing and improving it? Some may argue that such an exercise requires justification. It is necessary to explore some issues here.

1.3 First, with respect to *improving* use, studies of this kind tend to elicit two distinct responses. On the one hand, there are those who welcome some attention to this issue, especially regarding research funded by government departments. As such departments can be assumed to fund research in order to make use of it, seeking means of increasing such use is viewed as long overdue. Most of those with whom we spoke fell in this camp. Some researchers were very proud of the extent to which their research had been used and eager to pass their experience on to others. Others had been discouraged by the lack of use made of their findings. Some users, at both central and local level, felt much could be done to improve use. There is undoubtedly wide support for looking at the problem.

1.4 A few researchers, however, are deeply suspicious of efforts to increase the use of funded research. They argue that an increasingly utilitarian approach to research is likely to prove detrimental to the growth of knowledge in a wider sense. Too much attention to the question of use is seen to be at the expense of other aims of research and to represent a 'philistine' approach to intellectual endeavour. It especially fails to recognise the much wider contribution which researchers can make. There is particular concern at what may be an increasingly narrow definition of what constitutes research use.

1.5 There tends to be more uncertainty about *assessing* research use. Some argue, very simply, that it cannot be done. To the extent that research is about developing a greater understanding of issues, changing the ways in which they are viewed, any assessment of the direct use of findings will miss the point. Use of research may be so subtle that no direct connection to a particular project can be traced. This makes any assessment of the use of results extremely difficult if not impossible. There is, in addition, concern that the process of assessing research use might lead to a reduction in the freedom of researchers to pursue apparently unfruitful avenues, as there may be no measurable impact from such work. It is argued that it is therefore inappropriate to try.

1.6 We undertook this exercise with a firm belief that it *was* worthwhile to try both to improve use and to assess it. Our discussions only served to confirm this view. While some research may prove of no immediate or direct use, it is certainly appropriate to look for ways of making all research as fully useful and used as possible, particularly where funded by a government department. Research will remain only one of many influences on those who make decisions, but it does them a service to seek ways of helping them to make greater use of research findings.

1.7 Regarding the assessment of use, we do not argue that utility should be the sole criterion for judging research, but it is certainly an important one – and one which has, surprisingly, not been given the attention it deserves. Its importance is underlined where public money has been spent and some means of accounting for the decisions made is required. Use of research findings should, however, be widely interpreted, as we explore below.

1.8 This is not to say that there are no inherent difficulties in assessing research use. It is very difficult to identify the use of research, partly because its effect is often long-term and indirect and partly because those using research are often unaware of the source of their ideas. Research may be used to decide *not* to take an issue further, with no visible evidence of that course. Furthermore, much research is in principle useful, but is not used because decisions are taken on other grounds. Assessing research use may, in effect, entail an assessment both of researchers and of users. All these considerations make assessment a difficult and potentially controversial exercise.

1.9 The key issue, of course, is what will be done with any information collected. This raises the larger question of what may be an underlying political agenda. Exercises of this kind may be – and may be seen to be – means of controlling or limiting public expenditure on research. We would argue strongly that they should not be accepted in this light. The amount spent on research is necessarily a *political* decision and should be seen to be so. Setting up systems to improve or assess the use of research may affect the *kind* of research funded, but it should not in itself affect the overall amount. Indeed, we believe that any assessment process may benefit research by demonstrating the extent to which findings are disseminated and used.

1.10 We return to these issues throughout this report; they underlie all our recommendations, both on assessing – and on improving – the dissemination and use of research.

Meanings of use

1.11 Probably the most complex issue which we have had to address is the meaning of *use* itself. The term is employed in different contexts and in varying ways. Our interest here lies in the use of research by public bodies, although there are many other users as explored more fully below (see paras 1.18 – 1.22).

1.12 The traditional view of research use is based on an assumption that research is undertaken expressly to have direct utility. It is commissioned by policy-makers in response to a perceived need for some information or analysis on a specific issue. When the results are received, they are readily welcomed and translated as soon as conveniently possible into changes in policy or practice. There is, it is assumed, a direct line from the commissioning stage through the undertaking and completion of research to the point at which results are 'taken on board' or, in simple terms, put to use.

1.13 This is a powerful model, which still holds sway in some circles. Indeed, it is an appropriate one in some circumstances. We would term this kind of use to be 'direct' use by customers. But it is increasingly recognised that action rarely proceeds quite so smoothly. As one writer in this field argues:

> '*Public officials use research . . . but they do not often use it by considering the findings of one study in the context of a specific pending decision and adopting the course of action recommended by (or derived directly from) the research.*'[1]

She offers many reasons why this is so, ranging from the technical to the political. Among the former, research often does not fit the exact circumstances in which a decision is to be taken, results may not reach the right audience or be available at the appropriate time and decision-makers may not know how to interpret or apply particular findings. Among the latter, decision-makers may not trust research findings; more significantly, the lessons are often outweighed by a combination of competing interests. It is also commonly argued that policy-makers do not work in the way assumed; they do not define goals and set priorities, but cope with day-to-day problems 'with the focus strictly on the here and now'.[2] In sum, direct use of research in the described manner is not all that common.

1.14 Yet researchers have not been slow to argue that the fact that research is not used directly does not mean that it is not used at all. They argue that the assumption of an immediate traceable impact from research to practice is misplaced. Research, they suggest, adds to the broad pool of knowledge accumulated over time from which those seeking understanding may occasionally sip. Another analogy here is the effect of water on limestone, with the implication that its course cannot readily be predicted: 'You may know where the water falls . . . [but not] what route it will take down the various levles or where it will emerge through unexpected fissures.'[3] The real benefits of research, it is suggested, lie in its ability to enhance long-term understanding or enlightenment.

1.15 We would argue that there are two distinct issues here–*when* research is used and *how* it is used. With regard to the timing, research may be used immediately and directly (the traditional view) or it may be used over a longer term but nonetheless directly, when the import of the results have become clearer or more pressing. With regard to how research is used, it may be used directly (immediately or long term) or indirectly, affecting broad understanding of a subject as described above.

1.16 Even the immediate use of research can take many different forms. For instance, research can be used to provide valuable background for pressing issues or confirm that decisions have been taken in roughly the right way. Research may elicit results which are in some sense already known, but which serve to validate existing knowledge. Some research helps to clarify ideas, pulling them together in a new and coherent way. Research, in short, often provides 'a background to decision-making

---

[1] Carol Hirshon Weiss, 'Knowledge creep and decision accretion', *Knowledge: Creation, Diffusion, Utilisation*, Vol 1, no 3, March 1980, p 396.

[2] Tim Booth, in *Developing Policy Research*, Aldershot: Gower, 1988, p 5; this book provides a useful introduction to these issues.

[3] Robin Guthrie, 'Research and Social Policy', paper delivered at the conference of researchers on violence in marriage, Bristol, 1979, quoted in Patricia Thomas, *The Aims and Outcomes of Social Policy Research*, London: Croom Helm, 1985, p 99.

rather than direct prescriptions for change.'[1] We note that one writer proposes a distinction between use and application; research is 'used' when it is given some attention – read, analysed, discussed or even suppressed – whereas it is 'applied' when its recommendations have some impact on decisions.[2] We do not employ this terminology, but it does help to point up the different stages involved in use.

1.17 What is essential here is to acknowledge that the use of research is not limited to the direct and immediate use by the customers who fund a study. There may be indirect use, long-term use and, in this context, use by others, such as local and health authorities and the many practitioners employed by them. Research is used when it helps to explicate a problem and develop broader understanding as well as when it has a direct impact on a pressing issue. All of these kinds of use should be viewed *as use* and all are important in different ways.

Research users

1.18 If research is intended to be used, the immediate question is by whom? There are, in fact, many different potential users of DH/DSS research. It should not be assumed that any one study has only one audience, nor that the audience for certain areas of inquiry is always the same. These can be discussed in terms of certain broad groups.

1.19 The principal audience of most government-funded research broadly comprises those working for or on behalf of public agencies. Most important among these is the sponsoring customer, responsible for devising and reflecting on policies and advising Ministers accordingly. But also important are their equivalent numbers in local and health authorities, that is people concerned with issues of local policy. Finally, mention should be made of those responsible for putting policies into practice, including a wide range of health and social service professionals at local level. We tend to use the term 'practitioners' to refer to this latter group.

1.20 But there are others with an interest in such research. Service users or the general public may well be interested in using some research where it is relevant to their particular problems or affects service delivery; they may also have a general intellectual curiosity about the results of research. Similarly, professional and training bodies may seek to incorporate research findings into their training. Voluntary organisations, including pressure groups, may use research findings to press their case, at both central and local level. Commercial organisations, especially where working in the fields of health and social care, may have a direct financial interest in the outcomes of some research. And use is also made of research by the media.

1.21 Finally, of course, academics, including other researchers as well as teachers, provide a major audience for much research, for use in their teaching as well as to feed into yet further research.

1.22 None of these audiences, of course, is monolithic. There are differences in perspective between different professional groups, between those working to different

---

[1] Peter Brannen, 'Research and social policy: political, organisational and cultural constraints', in Frank Heller (ed), *The Use and Abuse of Social Science*, Sage, London, p 159.

[2] This distinction is discussed by Tim Booth, *op cit*, p 240.

departments or divisions, between lay and professional people and so forth. Moreover, within any one group, there will be differences in views and concerns, arising from varying perspectives about the problem under discussion and different emphases given to conflicting values.

Kinds of research

1.23 Anyone involved in research knows that the term is used to cover many different kinds of activity and the type of research clearly affects research use. Research may be classified on a number of different dimensions. We believe the principal ones of relevance to this exercise are the purpose of the research and its subject matter.[1]

1.24 The purpose of research necessarily affects not only the type of research 'output' but the audience to which it is addressed and the degree to which use is likely to be direct or more diffuse. There are six main (not always mutually exclusive) categories of policy-relevant research[2]:

1.25 Contextual or descriptive research provides some current information on a problem, such as the number of people with Alzheimer's disease, the number of local authorities with a specific policy on AIDS or the educational qualifications of those working in social security offices. It may be defined as 'intelligence', providing the basic information on which further questions can be asked or decisions taken.

1.26 Diagnostic or analytical research goes beyond simple description to attempt an explanation of phenomena, to work through careful examination to discover what is popularly known as cause and effect. Some relevant examples would be an explanation of changes in the birth rate, research on the reasons for the development of self-help groups or a consideration of variations in benefit take-up. Such research provides some basis for understanding not simply what the current position is but why it has come to be so.

1.27 Strategic research is directed toward discovery of the implications of particular plans, assessing alternatives and finding solutions; in some circles, this is referred to as option analysis. It might entail, for instance, an analysis of the numbers at risk from universal vaccination programmes, a consideration of the form which a new carers' centre might take or an examination of the political implications of a change in the benefit system.

1.28 Evaluative research is intended to assess the benefits and costs of a particular programme or course of action to those directly involved and the wider community. For example, it might involve testing a new drug, evaluating an initiative to help elderly people remain at home or assessing the effectiveness of working practices at DSS local office level.

---

[1] We note that the Cabinet Office, *Annual Review of Government Funded R&D* in 1986 categorised research in terms of four outcomes: basic, applied, strategic and experimental development. The subsequent report in 1987 proposed seven 'primary purpose' categories. We prefer the classification system used here.

[2] This classification is based mainly on Jane Ritchie 'A perspective on the application of qualitative research to social policy' in Jane Ritchie and Wendy Sykes (eds), *Advanced Workshop in Applied Qualitative Research*, Social and Community Planning Research, 1986.

1.29 Developmental research is intended to study the processes of implementation of a specific programme, including its initial development and design, with a concern to feed back information to enable that programme to be changed. It is sometimes referred to as 'action research'. For instance, it might involve monitoring an anti-smoking campaign, a case management project for people with disabilities or the introduction of computers into DSS local offices – in all three cases if information were immediately made available to consider changes in the programme in question.

1.30 Methodological research is concerned to assess existing methods and techniques and develop new ones for understanding certain kinds of substantive questions. This can be of central importance in enabling research to be taken further. For example, it might involve finding new means of diagnosing particular diseases, breaking new ground in methods of evaluating social programmes or assessing the bases for determining the numbers of unemployed people.

1.31 The audiences for each of these kinds of information are likely to differ. Thus, contextual research is likely to have a wide audience, including people concerned with policy and practice and the wider academic community. Strategic research, on the other hand, tends to be targeted primarily at those concerned directly with policy or practice. Developmental research will be of particular concern to those directly involved and methodological research will be of primary interest to other researchers.

1.32 The points in the policy process at which various kinds of information is sought are also likely to differ from one kind of study to another. Methodological research, for instance, is essentially a means of establishing the foundations on which further research can be based. Strategic research, similarly, is important at the outset of a programme when considering how to take it further. In contrast, evaluative research is a means of looking back on how such programmes developed over time. Contextual and diagnostic research may prove of use at many stages of the policy process.

1.33 Research can also be classified by broad subject area, for instance, social security, nursing, primary health care and so forth. Such a classification might also extend to whether research is *for* the professionals in question (for example, nurses) and therefore about practice and service delivery issues or *about* the professional group and therefore about broader policy issues. Both kinds of subject classifications affect the audience for the research and have some relevance to practical issues, such as the number and kinds of outlets available for dissemination.

Research and researchers

1.34 Last, but not least, there is a need to address briefly the territory under discussion – what is 'research'? This term, as has been shown, covers a wide range of exercises devoted in some way or other to finding something out. Individual studies vary enormously. We have explored briefly how their aims, subjects and audiences differ. They may also vary in their methods – having a quantitative or qualitative approach, involving fieldwork or desk research and collecting new information or using existing data. In addition, research projects differ considerably in their size, from a single researcher to a large research team. These are not matters which need to be explored in detail here.

1.35 This exercise was initially undertaken with a focus on issues surrounding the various products of such research, including publications, personal communications or other means of dissemination. But research – in terms of what researchers do and the kind of contribution they are able to make – may extend beyond the products of individual research projects to the use of researchers themselves. Researchers are people who are employed to think. They tend to develop a deep view about the issues they study and, at best, the ability to bring an analytical perspective to bear on new problems. Indeed, this may extend beyond their specific inquiries to an ability to provide valuable illumination on other issues altogether. The use of research can therefore be seen to encompass the use of researchers themselves as well as the specific products of their work.

Assumptions of this study

1.36 We have set out a range of distinctions and clarifications here to provide a context for the discussion in the following chapters. We must also add a few comments about the assumptions we have made about the weight of DH/DSS interest.

1.37 Following our brief, we have assumed that the research under consideration here comprises the many studies commissioned by the Research Management Divisions[1] of the DS/DSS in the fields of health, personal social services and social security (referred to internally at the start of our project as HPSS/SS). These cover a very wide range. In 1987/88, there were 33 units and programmes based in universities, NHS authorities and other institutions, and over 300 individual projects; expenditure for directly managed research in this area amounted to £13.6m.[2]

1.38 We have assumed that we should consider means of assessing and improving the dissemination and use of *all* the research currently (or potentially) funded, in other words covering studies involving all aims and all subject areas noted. We have also assumed that in considering means of improving research use, we should look at the use of both the products of research and, to a lesser degree, researchers themselves. With respect to the kind of use, we have assumed that the principal concern lies in assessing and improving the direct use of research results, although there is nonetheless some considerable interest in indirect and long-term use.

1.39 But we have also assumed that our exercise was not intended to be targeted at all potential users of research. We viewed the prime interest, with respect both to improving and assessing research use, to be use by public agencies, at both central and local level. Thus, we consider use both by the DH/DSS themselves and by those concerned with policy or practice in local and health authorities. We give little attention to means of increasing the use of research by other academics, commercial organisations or the general public.

1.40 Finally, we undertook this exercise on the assumption that the scientific merit or quality of research results were outside our remit. Although we make an occasional mention of this issue where appropriate, all recommendations had to be based on an assumption that research is 'worth' disseminating and using.

---

[1] We use this term generically throughout this report to refer to those carrying out research management functions within both Departments, although only the Department of Health retains the name.

[2] DHSS, *Handbook of Research and Development 1988*, London: HMSO.

1.41 We might add here that some DH/DSS-funded researchers have more than one source of funding. Although the outcomes from such work are not within the purview of the DH/DSS, in some cases it may be difficult to disentangle the appropriate information.

1.42 Having set this context, it is possible to turn to specific recommendations. In the concluding chapter, we return to some of the issues raised here.

Getting Research out: Improving Dissemination

2.1 Research cannot be used unless it is available to those who might use it. This chapter is concerned with getting research out or, more formally, *dissemination*. It explores ways in which the dissemination of DH/DSS research might be improved.

2.2 There is a need to begin, however, by exploring briefly both the many ways in which researchers currently do disseminate and a diagnosis of the problem – why dissemination is less satisfactory than it should be. We should add that in identifying some problems, we do not wish to imply that they are universal. There is undeniably a lot of variation in dissemination patterns; we have no systematic evidence on the issue.

Current modes of dissemination

2.3 Research is disseminated in a wide variety of ways. Through our discussions, we found that many researchers had been highly imaginative in seeking out channels for communicating their results. Some only responded to opportunities as they arose, but others planned their dissemination very carefully from the start. Some researchers, perhaps surprisingly, did not seem to appreciate that such activity outside their laboratory or library could reasonably be judged to be part of the research enterprise.

2.4 Dissemination to the Department must be addressed first. The submission of a final report is generally the first task on completion of a project. In some cases, this is preceded by papers, interim reports or other documentation to customers or RMD during the course of the research. Some researchers noted that they had also helped the Department to prepare guidance documents, codes of practice and other practical publications. A few had been asked for material to help customers prepare answers to Parliamentary Questions or briefings to Ministers. Some had also submitted evidence to Government or Parliamentary Committees.

2.5 Secondly, there is dissemination to researchers' academic peers and a wider intellectual audience, through the publication of one or more books or articles in academic journals. Some researchers help to produce in-house research journals. Many noted that they had given papers to academic conferences and were generally involved in a wide academic network, both national and international. Such work included refereeing the work of other researchers (both for publication and for funding), sitting on research advisory committees both for the Department(s) and the Research Councils, participating in a Chief Scientist's Visit to units and undertaking other forms of academic inspection and validation. All were perceived as aspects of spreading knowledge gained from research.

2.6 Many researchers are also university teachers and disseminate their research findings through their teaching. Those who are not so employed are often invited to give lectures both at their own insitution and elsewhere. Research is also disseminated to students through its incorporation in undergraduate textbooks.

2.7 Third, much dissemination is directed to those concerned with local policy and practice. Many researchers make a particular effort to publish articles in the relevant trade journals, such as *Nursing Times, Community Care* and *Nursery World*, to give some examples. A few have turned academic books into texts for practitioners. Many have given considerable time to both conferences and individual talks for local policy-makers and practitioners. Some have done 'roadshows' about their work; one told us she tended to do one talk a week.

2.8 A number of researchers spend a lot of time, in the words of one, 'embedding research in the local community'. They work closely with district or regional health authorities, community health councils and local authority departments. They sit on specialist advisory panels, work with practitioners to test and refine findings and generally assist in the development of relevent local schemes. Some have close working relations with key officers or managers, for instance in health promotion or planning. In a similar vein, some have designed educational and training materials or contributed to special training programmes. Some have helped to train trainers. Where any such involvement is used to gain access to data, a conscious effort is generally made to feed back results to those involved.

2.9 Fourth, attachment to and involvement with professional associations and colleges provides yet another mechanism for research dissemination, especially where such bodies provide in-service training or guidance on practice for their members. This is particularly significant with respect to specialisms in the medical field.

2.10 Fifth, some researchers are involved with voluntary bodies with a research or service interest in their field (for instance Cancer Research Campaign, Mencap, Child Poverty Action Group) in much the same way as the involvement with statutory bodies already described. In some cases, these organisations serve as the source of data and, occasionally, provide supplementary funding. A number of researchers said they were active on specialist committees of such organisations, advising on new schemes and experiments. Some also produced training packs, guidance for operational staff, videos and pamphlets.

2.11 Where such groups act in a pressure group capacity, however, researchers tend to be reluctant to become too involved. A few noted that they had had a poor experience relating to the misuse of their findings; others were simply wary of such a possibility. But many researchers recognise the valuable role that such groups can play on behalf of their constituencies. This could be particularly critical for research dissemination, where organisations have sophisticated publicity machinery and distribution arrangements for publications.

2.12 Sixth, there is the wider public. While the great majority of researchers we spoke to did not attempt to target their findings beyond fairly clearly specified audiences, there were notable exceptions. Some had written books for service consumers generally or people with particular problems. Some had published in other popular outlets, such as women's magazines. Many had taken part at one time or another in radio or television programmes. Although there was considerable reluctance to seek coverage in the national press, a few had had feature articles published about their research, written either by themselves or specialist journalists. Some found the local press receptive to information about their research – and this a useful means of getting to local people.

2.13 Finally, some researchers extend their dissemination activities to work with international agencies, such as the World Health Organisation and the EEC.

2.14 Most researchers interviewed seemed to want an active role in disseminating their findings; many, indeed, suggested that they would like to do more. They expressed a personal commitment to such work, not primarily to advance their careers or the reputation of their institution but to enable others to benefit from their conclusions. This was especially the case where they saw clear steps which might improve the lives of those whose problems their research had addressed. Commitment was also expressed to the wider academic and professional communities.

2.15 The amount of help given by the DH/DSS in these efforts seems to vary enormously. Some customers take an active interest in dissemination and discuss with researchers what might be done with their work. Some also make an explicit effort to pass on reports both to their immediate colleagues and to others outside, for instance in NHS Regions. The role of liaison officers also seems to vary. Some have played a highly active role in suggesting ideas for dissemination, facilitating conferences and providing funds towards publication; others seem to do very little in this way. Such interest was almost always very welcome from the research end.

Some problems

2.16 But few people question that there are also problems with dissemination. This is partly a matter of the *amount*; there is a widespread feeling that research findings are not disseminated as much as they could be. In addition, there are problems of targeting the right audiences – getting the *right kind* of dissemination, addressed to those with a real interest in the results. These problems are best explored in terms of professional and practical considerations.

2.17 There are two distinct professional issues here. One is whether researchers have a sense of responsibility for dissemination. While most of the researchers we spoke to did consider dissemination to be their job, a few clearly did not. Some simply lacked enthusiasm for the work; they found the process of finding out interesting but the process of transmitting results to others more pedestrian. Others felt that too much interest in the outcomes of their research might prejudice their objectivity. Some were also reluctant to expose their data to audiences who might use them inappropriately, for instance taking information out of context to make a political point. There was some reluctance to engage in any activity that would force them to simplify their findings.

2.18 The second issue relates to professional recognition; many researchers feel they are given little credit for dissemination outside the normal academic framework. For those within a university setting, their future career may be at stake. Publication in a peer-referred journal is the normal route to promotion. Dissemination to other groups is not felt to count for very much.

2.19 But this problem also extends to researchers in other contexts. The ability of *all* researchers to gain funding for further research from the DS/DSS is seen to depend largely on an academic assessment of their work. This is particularly visible in the case of research units, where the Chief Scientist's Visit seems to stress scientific quality and not give much attention to other beneficial outcomes of the work. The fact that the research may be widely known or influential seems to hold little weight. Some researchers questioned the extent to which the DH/DSS took any interest in dissemination beyond their own walls. Several spoke of reports disappearing into a 'black hole', receiving only cursory or pedantic comments. Many did not know whether, how and to whom their work had been circulated – nor had they been asked for any interim papers.

2.20 Some researchers told us that early dissemination – before the production of a report – had been actively discouraged. A few had even chosen not to disclose all the dissemination they had carried out for fear that it would count against them in some way. The 1987 research contract, requiring the consent of the Secretary of State prior to publication, was seen as further evidence of lack of interest in dissemination. Some noted that scientific journals were said to look less favourably now on submissions arising from DH/DSS-funded research because of a fear that the findings had been in some way censored. This was a clear source of concern.

2.21 On the practical side, the main problems for dissemination are lack of time and resources. This often begins at the proposal writing stage; many researchers underestimate the time required for a project in order to secure funding in the first place. In any case, there is a tendency – even among experienced researchers – to underestimate writing-up time. The contract period thus often includes only minimal time for writing and rarely assumes time for other dissemination. When projects are nearing completion, researchers are almost inevitably concerned about their next job or contract; anxiety at this time tends to inhibit creative thinking about dissemination. Indeed, where there are fixed term contracts, the research team tends to break up at this point, as each member follows his or her own career interests. Considerable expertise is lost where key researchers go on to another job.

2.22 Once a project has been completed, and a report submitted, there are normally no further resources for dissemination to other audiences. Indeed, researchers are then employed to do other work altogether. Several researchers felt there was an unwritten assumption that they could write a book from a previous project in their evenings or weekends: 'they feel if you're good, you'll write anyway, you'll survive.' They argued that they were expected to do dissemination but not provided the necessary financial support. Many felt overburdened, trying to fit dissemination around other commitments, and angry about such assumptions affecting their lives.

2.23 There are also other resource limitations. A lack of administrative or clerical back-up to facilitate dissemination can create problems; it is difficult to organise a conference or produce new material in the absence of such support.

2.24 Some researchers told us that they lacked the skills to undertake wider dissemination. They found it difficult to simplify, summarise and popularise either in writing or orally in order to meet the needs of audiences other than the academic. Some felt they need training in these areas, as well as in dealing directly with the media to publicise work undertaken. Most had limited familiarity with using the media outside the written word.

2.25 Finally, in some fields there may be insufficient outlets for dissemination. The paucity of trade journals in some areas, the demise of the independent New Society and the lack of an equivalent to the Department of Employment Gazette were all noted here. Some researchers suggested that it was becoming increasingly difficult to get books published, especially those of minority interest, because of a growing centralisation in the publishing world. What has come to be called 'grey literature' – monographs, reports and the like – are not readily published and often require some initial financial outlay. In some specialisms, increased competition – as well as biasses in favour of certain kinds of research – was said to make publication in reputable journals difficult. Pressure to publish with HMSO was not always welcome. Copyright problems may also discourage publication in some cases. It was also said to be harder to get publicity or reviews because of increased competition.

2.26 While many of these difficulties stem from problems at the researchers' end, some arise from barriers within the DH/DSS. In some cases it is clear that there is no Departmental interest in wide dissemination of the findings. This is more common in the DSS, which commissions some studies primarily for internal use. In addition, some customers feel they have no time for dissemination and do not view it as their responsibility. Perhaps more significantly, the role of RMD, serving in one customer's words as 'a professional filter', is often unclear, with insufficient attention given to dissemination of research. As noted above, there appears to be wide variation between liaison officers in the interest taken in such activity.

Establishing a strategy for dissemination

2.27 Of all the recommendations made here, probably the most central is the need to give dissemination greater *legitimacy*. Researchers – and others who might help them disseminate their findings – need to feel that time allocated to this task is time properly spent. Dissemination needs to be viewed as part of what researchers do – indeed, one central part of the wider process of planning and executing research projects. This means giving explicit attention to dissemination from the outset of a study. Researchers, research managers and customers should be fully agreed on the products which are expected to flow from it.

2.28 What we are proposing here is a *strategic* approach to dissemination. This needs to come from within the Department(s), beginning with their respective Research Management Divisions[1]. There is a need to stress the importance of dissemination, welcome time and resources spent on dissemination activities and give support to researchers as needed for work on such tasks. A commitment to dissemination needs to be spelled out and discussed with researchers themselves. A strategic approach should entail setting up the appropriate organisational structures and working arrangements to enable dissemination to take place and ensuring that sufficient resources are available.

Encouraging dissemination

2.29 Researchers should be seen to have principal responsibility for dissemination. With a few exceptions, this is their own view, arising from their unique familiarity with their results and capacity to explain them. They argue, in one researcher's words: 'the Department can't disseminate my research, but it should make it possible for me to do so'. Researchers should be encouraged to write dissemination activities into their research proposals and to budget accordingly. This would help to clarify the full period required by a study and reduce the tendency to underestimate the time it may

---

[1] As noted in the previous chapter, we use this term generically to refer to those carrying out research management functions.

take. Where proposals are put out to tendering, costing for dissemination time should be welcomed and not prejudice the proposal.

2.30 The other side of responsibility is giving credit to researchers for dissemination undertaken. Their efforts in this regard should be fully noted. Both RMD and customers should seek to commend researchers who actively disseminate their work. Decisions to fund further work should be taken – and be seen to be taken – in part on researchers' willingness to make their work well known in a useful way. The dissemination database proposed in chapter 4 would prove very helpful here (see paras 4.19 – 4.37).

2.31 The role of Research Management Division is particularly crucial here. It needs to take a lead in advising on dissemination. A clear responsibility for such advice should be part of the job specification of all liaison officers. They should be expected to think about appropriate means of disseminating the work for which they are responsible, to discuss these with researchers and customers and to seek out the resources for such activity. Time should be allocated for such tasks and there should be a sense of pressure to engage in them. In other words, dissemination should be seen as a key part of their job, along with the development of well designed projects and their management.[1] We return to wider issues about the role of liaison officers in the concluding chapter (see paras 5.31 – 5.60).

2.32 Customers should also take a more active role here. They should be encouraged to think of dissemination of the research which they fund as an activity deserving their attention. They should advise researchers on new audiences for their findings and recommend support for dissemination as appropriate. Some customers are highly conscious of their need to limit dissemination, for instance not approving a publication deemed to be poor. We cannot argue over this, but it regrettably casts a major cloud over any dissemination policy, probably quite out of proportion to the number of times it occurs. It would be helpful if customers could take a more proactive stance in the other direction in the many cases where it is warranted.

2.33 Many researchers could use advice on dissemination – about where to publish their findings to reach new audiences, how to turn a heavy, academic text into a more readable document or even very detailed practical advice, such as how to write a press release. Some could use training in public speaking or in using the media. The DH/DSS press office might be able to help here, for instance organising a seminar on some of these issues.

2.34 A strategic approach means giving attention to the kinds of audiences which would benefit from a particular study and then thinking about how to get to them. While there are many different groups potentially interested in research findings, the primary concern of the DH/DSS is likely to be dissemination to public agencies. This should be widely interpreted to include both the initial customers and those responsible for policy and practice at local level. The latter, as we explore below, can prove a very important audience for research findings.

---

[1] We note, for instance, that the 'trawl notice' for a Principal Research Officer (liaison officer) makes no mention of responsibility for dissemination, but stresses the 'development and management' of research.

2.35 As it is rarely possible to meet the needs of all audiences in one document, it is necessary for researchers to produce more than one kind of output – putting what one researcher called 'a lot of bait into many different ponds.' This should be not only at the end of a study but, where appropriate, throughout its course. We discuss below some specific ideas about differing kinds of dissemination (see paras 2.72 – 2.90) and in the following chapter we consider how to make research findings salient to different audiences (see paras 3.51 – 3.53 and 3.71 – 3.72).

Looking at the research contract

2.36 Dissemination arrangements should be formalised by writing the expected products from a study into the research contract. This should state the kind of publications and other outputs which are envisaged and the time at which they are to be produced. The resources allocated to the project should be sufficient to cover these outputs. Thus, for example, a contract might state that the researcher is expected to produce a book, an article in a practitioner journal and one conference paper by a specified date. Interim publications might also be noted here. Additional outputs should be encouraged through a contingency clause to cover such work as appropriate.

2.37 It is essential for such a specification to be reviewed at some point. At the outset of a study, it is inevitably difficult to judge exactly whom a subject will interest, especially as researchers can shift their focus, quite appropriately, mid-stream. A piece of research may also acquire much greater topicality than initially anticipated. Dissemination should be considered at some predetermined point during every project. This might be via an advisory group or through more informal discussion between researchers, customers and the liaison officer. Clear decisions should then be taken about what dissemination is to be attempted and at what time. A fuller dissemination phase might also be negotiated at this point (see para 2.44).

2.38 In discussing the research contract, it must be noted that many researchers are deeply concerned about the 1987 change requiring prior approval before publication. It is feared that this will not only limit their ability to publish but that researchers will also increasingly engage in self-censorship to avoid argument. We understand that fairly amicable agreement about the meaning of the contract has been achieved with the researchers most directly concerned. Researchers need to be reassured that they will genuinely be able to publish their uncensored findings and to disseminate them in other ways. The contract states that 'consent shall not be unreasonably withheld'; it will be important for researchers to see that this is so. If there are subjects on which publication is expected to be problematic, this should be discussed with researchers from the outset.

Other incentive systems

2.39 While specifying outputs in a contract serves as a mild incentive system for researchers by setting clear targets, there are much stronger measures which could be applied. The final payment on a contract could be tied to the completion of agreed products – whether a final report or other publications. This would affect not only the researchers involved but also, perhaps subjecting them to even greater pressure, their employing institution. We note that such a specification currently exists in the standard research contract, but are not certain whether the intended threat has ever been carried out. It should be clearly stated that funding of further research is contingent on the completion of all agreed products.

2.40 Researchers should also be assessed in part on their dissemination record. Referees, both of initial proposals and of finished reports, should be explicitly asked to comment on the amount and appropriateness of researchers' dissemination activities. RMD should ensure that they have full information on this matter. Dissemination should also be addressed during Chief Scientist Visits (see paras 4.56 – 4.57 for a fuller discussion of this issue).

Increasing the resources available for dissemination

2.41 As with most activities, an increase in the resources directed to research dissemination would make a significant impact on the amount undertaken. 'Resources' should be seen to include not only hard cash expressly for this activity but also the specification of time to be spent in this way under existing budgets.

2.42 The need for additional funding for dissemination seems to us very clear. Dissemination is important and funds should be available for it. The real question here is not *whether* such funding should be available but *by what means*.

Funding researchers for dissemination

2.43 There are two kinds of dissemination costs: the direct costs incurred in travel, organising conferences, publication and so forth, and researchers' *time*. At present, researchers themselves – and their employing institutions – tend to bear all such costs. Some researchers find a heavy imposition on their own time; some serve as virtual information centres on their subject. One vividly described projects as having a 'half life' during which some interest continues in the work. The more researchers disseminate, of course, the more the demands made on them. We cannot see why researchers should be required to meet these costs themselves.

2.44 A clear dissemination period should be established for research projects as appropriate. This should be a set amount of time after the completion of the research, when the time and expenses of researchers directed to dissemination are paid for. The appropriate period would vary between projects, determined perhaps roughly at the outset and more specifically when the research is complete. It might be up to a week (five researcher days) over the year after completion, for discussions with customers and writing a short article. Alternatively, it might be one month (20 days) to enable the researcher to undertake extensive writing, set up a conference or carry out 'roadshows' to discuss the work.

2.45 Such arrangements would need to be specified in writing and discussed carefully with the researchers involved. It would be important to guard against encroachment on such dissemination time. If ordinary research time 'slipped' by this amount, as some see as highly likely, then the researchers should be said to be in default of their contract and to owe that time. If a researcher continued not to meet agreed deadlines, the allocation of further contracts would need to be given careful attention. No arrangement is foolproof, but we suspect that contracts of this kind can be made to work and would be highly welcomed by the research community.

2.46 This proposal would most easily be implemented in the case of research units and programmes. Here, there is an expectation of continuity with the researchers and it should be fairly simple to specify a proportion of budgets for dissemination time. Indeed, it seems surprising that, at present, the standard contract for research units makes no reference to dissemination activities as part of the expenditure covered. Attention should be given to rectifying this situation.

2.47 But such an arrangement, with some exceptions, should also be possible with researchers on one-off projects. Many of these continue to carry out research when the one contract has ended and many are in any case academics with a continuing interest in the field. The key problem is rarely lack of interest, but the need for payment for time given to dissemination activity.

2.48 One variant of the dissemination period, which may only be feasible in the case of funded units, is to indicate in the research contract that a set (small) proportion of the time for one study may be given to dissemination of earlier projects, from whatever funding source. This would need to be additional time, that is over and above what would have been specified for the work. This arrangement is similar to a dissemination period, but provides a more open remit. Some units and researchers operate such a system *de facto* at present. We believe that it would be better for such arrangements to be more open and explicit.

2.49 Finally, where the employment of a research translator (see paras 2.53 – 2.64) is under consideration, researchers might be given first option on their task, with an in-built financial incentive. Research translators are employed to turn research findings into more popular publications. It clearly costs some money to hire them. An equivalent sum could be made available as an inducement at the end of a study to those researchers who produce work which does not require such translation. This should increase the production of readable publications without the hassle of employing an outsider, although some difficulties in adjudication might arise here.

A central dissemination budget

2.50 In addition to resources allocated in advance for researchers, RMD should have a budget specifically designated for dissemination. Liaison officers should be able to use such funds to facilitate the dissemination of research results once projects are completed. We understand that some funds can be found at present by RMD from the general research fund, but these are not explicitly earmarked for the one purpose. Such a central fund should be well publicised to both researchers and customers.

2.51 This budget could be used for a variety of purposes. It might help to pay the initial costs of a publication or the direct costs of conferences, seminars and workshops. It should also be used, as appropriate, to pay for researchers' time. Such an arrangement is very flexible. It makes it possible to cope with the inevitably uneven demands on researchers, which can be especially heavy when a book is published (often long after the work is finished) or if their work becomes highly topical (which may be at any time). Such flexibility should be viewed as a considerable bonus, as there need be little waste. We might add that such funds should be viewed as open to being used to disseminate research not initially funded by the Department(s), where the work is felt to be valuable and within their broad research remit.

Special arrangements for dissemination

2.52 Increasing the resources available for dissemination is not only a matter of specifying funds for this purpose. There are a range of organisational and other arrangements which might be set up to facilitate the dissemination of research findings.

Research interpreters

2.53 The employment of a research interpreter or translator is one means of increasing dissemination. This is someone with sufficient understanding of research to comprehend findings in full, but who is able to summarise arguments to make them accessible to the non-academic reader. He or she might be a specialist journalist, for instance in the medical or social work fields, or someone with a relevant professional background who also has entrepreneurial and writing skills.

2.54 There are a number of jobs which a research interpreter might undertake. One is the preparation of articles for the professional trade press or more popular journals, such as women's magazines. Another is preparing training materials or practical guidebooks, translating research findings into specific recommendations for in-service training or practical action. In some cases, the interpreter might synthesize the results of more than one project, bringing together a range of findings in a general field or specialism.

2.55 One example here is the exercise carried out in the mid-1980s for the DHSS concerning children in care, often referred to as the 'pink book' exercise. A large DHSS-funded research programme on the subject came to fruition at the same time as work funded by the ESRC. A joint committee was set up, including customers, researchers, research managers and representatives of the ESRC, chaired by the Deputy Chief Inspector of the Social Services Inspectorate. A group of middle managers from Social Services Departments were asked by the committee to pull out the implications of this research for their work.

2.56 A research interpreter, with both research and practical experience, was hired to produce a publication based on the research material (the 'pink book'). This provided an overview of the research, summarised the findings of individual projects and synthesised common themes and arguments. In addition, exercises to enable users to test the research findings against their own experience were set out.[1] To coincide with the report's publication, a national conference of Social Services Directors and Chairmen of Social Services Committees was organised. This was followed by a series of regional seminars, intended to establish a system of 'networking' whereby key people would spread ideas to others in their local area. Various training bodies were also awarded grants to incorporate the research findings into training.

2.57 We have heard many discussions of this exercise, for the most part favourable. It seems fortuitous that the different research projects produced similar messages for practice. The research reports were said to have been well written and to provide good anecdotal material. The part played by the research interpreter was clearly essential; she was felt to be both highly competent and acceptable to the researchers and practitioners taking part. The involvement of the SSI gave the exercise considerable status and facilitated dissemination to a wide audience. The practical exercises were widely thought to be helpful. A number of people in the field suggested the exercise had affected their thinking on the subject and customers were also very enthusiastic.

---

[1] DHSS, *Social Work Decisions in Child Care: recent research findings and their implications*, London: HMSO, 1986.

Certainly, the book is well known to both practitioners and researchers; it has been reprinted three times.

2.58 In passing, it might be added that the regional conferences, in contrast to the initial national one, were not widely regarded as a success. Different explanations have been given here. The original research interpreter was not involved and the consultants hired for the task may not have been properly briefed. The networking exercise was said to be under-resourced, to have created a lot of paperwork and to have had little impact. Some suggested it had never been a good idea. Difficulties were also experienced in the attempts to translate the ideas into suitable training material.

2.59 Another model here is the employment of a research liaison officer expressly for dissemination. This, too, has been tried. It formed part of a wider initiative in the early 1980s by the Under Fives Research Dissemination Group, itself set up to discuss means of disseminating research sponsored by a number of government departments as well as the then Social Science Research Council (now ESRC). That initiative also resulted in the publication of a handbook incorporating summaries of individual research projects as well as the commissioning of wider research reviews for publication. These publications also proved highly popular.

2.60 The liaison officer in this case was employed to take a proactive approach to dissemination. It was argued that the onus of responsibility for learning about research should be shifted from individual practitioners to someone with a specific brief to help. It was the job of the liaison officer to familiarise herself with the reports and other writings from an initial set of projects, to discuss these with the researchers involved and then to find means of communicating more directly with those who would find them useful. Contact was made with the latter by a variety of methods, from an initial circular to personal contacts and networks. Various dissemination events across the country were then planned in response to their requests.

2.61 A report was produced by the liaison officer on her work, providing details of the audiences and subjects involved as well as some comments on participants' views of the exercise.[1] She felt it had been highly successful, reaching a wide range of audiences with very positive feedback. Indeed, at the end of the appointed time, there were considerable outstanding demands for her services. Several key aspects of the work were noted, including the view of the liaison officer as a 'resource', the ability to tailor dissemination to individual groups and the avoidance of an advocacy stance.

2.62 Yet another model for employing research interpreters is their attachment, perhaps on a part-time basis, to some of the larger research units. They would become highly familiar with the issues in the unit's field as well as their implications for potential users. The funding for such posts might derive, wholly or in part, from RMD.

2.63 The idea of employing research interpreters is not without its critics. Some academics argue that only a researcher could fully understand their conclusions and that, in particular, such a task could not be carried out by a journalist. They also suggest that to summarise is to do damage to the complexities of an issue, findings

---

[1] Denise Hevey, *Linking Research and Practice: the experience of a research liaison officer*, ESRC, 1984.

being easily distorted. On the other hand, some noted that they have seen such a role undertaken with no objection.

2.64 RMD should give serious attention to the circumstances where the employment of a research interpreter might prove beneficial. It may be especially useful when the findings from a number of related studies emerge at the same time. Should interpreters be appointed, there will remain a clear need for considerable discussion between the interpreter and the researchers involved and the ability to negotiate the final product. There is also a need for selectivity, both between projects and between the findings of any one project.

Vehicles for publicising research

2.65 Another dissemination resource are journals aimed at publicising research results. Some attention might be given to extending their number. There seems to be a particular dearth in the social security field; some see this as a problem also in the field of social care. If a new journal were to be introduced, it could be used to report both the conclusions of completed research and research in progress. Both the Department of Employment Gazette and the Home Office Research Bulletin were noted as useful examples here. Indeed, the former had been used to publish some research results because there was no other appropriate outlet.

2.66 We cannot recommend the introduction of a new journal (or journals) without much more detailed information about likely sales and readership, but the idea deserves further exploration. The Departments should also explore new kinds of arrangements with publishers, forgoing royalties in some cases for instance, to help to get material out.

2.67 Abstracting services, providing short descriptions of books, articles and other research outputs, seem to be highly welcome at many levels. Bulletins with such information are currently provided by the DH/DSS library for certain subject areas, such as health services, social services and nursing research, for both internal use and to outside users on a subscription basis.[1] The information is now also available on-line to subscribers, on a system called DHSS-DATA, including information dating back to 1983 and earlier in some cases.[2] We suspect this service is not widely known and more effort should be put into publicising it. We also suggest that research in progress might be included; such information is readily available within RMD, as it is collected for the R&D Handbook.

2.68 One difficulty with abstracts, of course, is the problem of information overload. So much is written that it is difficult for hard-pressed customers or local managers to know how to pick and choose. This suggests a need for an abstracting service with an evaluative component, identifying books or articles which are particularly useful and why. Such activity would not be appropriate for government departments, but it should be feasible for some enterprising researchers. An annotated listing of recent publications, much like the guides to current cinema provided by some magazines,

---

[1] A full list can be supplied by the DH Library, Alexander Fleming House, Elephant and Castle, London SE1 6BY.

[2] For further information, contact DATA-STAR, 5th floor, The Plaza Suite, 114 Jermyn Street, London SW1Y 6HJ; tel (01) 930 5503.

would save an enormous amount of time for readers across the country. We suspect it could prove highly popular for this reason.

2.69 Much more could also be done by RMD to publicise the existence of its research. Both the 'pink book' exercise and the Under Fives dissemination project mentioned above were partly popular for the easy accessibility they afforded to information on research. Other such books, in other fields, should be commissioned on a regular basis.

2.70 The annual R&D Handbook is itself not widely known. It should be better publicised, especially at local level. Equally importantly, it is not well organised for obtaining information on specific subject areas. We suggest that research should be listed not by funded institution but by research field. This is the format of the equivalent publication from the Home Office and it is immediately possible to see what work is under way in particular areas; the relevant liaison officer for the research is also listed.[1] If a dissemination database is established, this information could be readily available from that source (see paras 4.19 – 4.37).

2.71 The Department(s) should devise means of publicising research reports to other Divisions and to their own researchers. The possibility of getting this information onto the existing library database should be examined. It has also been suggested that recent reports might be advertised in trade journals.

Taking a hard look at types of dissemination

2.72 The many kinds of dissemination undertaken by researchers are described at the outset of this chapter and do not need to be repeated here. But not all researchers take an active stance in this way. Researchers need to take a good look at how they disseminate their findings. On the whole, the need is *not* for new kinds of dissemination but for those who do not currently do much to learn from those who do.

The written word

2.73 Publications are widely viewed to be the principal means by which people learn about research results. Publications, especially books, endure. They can be referred to over many years. Most researchers seek to produce some kind of published material, particularly academic articles or books, where possible.

2.74 Many researchers may need encouragement, however, to publish findings outside the normal academic networks. This is particularly important to get results to the many people concerned with policy and practice in local and health authorities. They rely on the principal trade journals. Although they tend to have limited time for reading, there is commonly a system – thought to be quite good by those with whom we talked – for ensuring that relevant articles are called to their attention. But such systems are predicated on an assumption that articles are written in the first place. We might add that this may not be such a problem in the case of medical practitioners, since they are more likely to read 'academic' journals, such as the *British Medical Journal*.

---

[1] Home Office Research and Planning Unit, *Research Programme 1988 – 89*, Home Office, London, 1989.

2.75 Some researchers need to be reminded to publish in such journals. The particular journals read within individual professions are well known. So, too, we suspect, are those by which those in local authority department research or planning sections try to keep up to date.[1] The more places a study is written up, we were told, the more credence it is likely to be given.

2.76 Researchers should also be encouraged to target their research to training needs, particularly in-service training. Trainers often use their own material; we were told they would welcome publications produced for their needs.

2.77 Where the material is suitable, researchers should also be invited to publish more widely, for instance in women's magazines and journals devoted to health issues. They might also write in the newsletters published by relevant voluntary organisations, which can prove quick means of reaching both service users and practitioners with an interest in the subject.

2.78 Some research units produce working papers; we do not know how widely these are read outside the academic community, although some customers seem to find them useful. Newsletters, in contrast, produced by some units with information about current research, were read and welcomed by people in the field.

2.79 Researchers should be required to produce summaries of their findings. These might consist of a single sheet or be somewhat longer (four or five pages, say); both kinds of summary can prove useful for different purposes. Such summaries should set out the principal findings and indicate how to gain further information. We note that a summary is currently required in the standard research contract, but are not certain whether this is always prepared. This deserves attention.

2.80 Summaries should not only be produced; they should also be widely distributed both by the researchers and by the Department(s) where appropriate. The current contract specifies the right of the Department to provide such summaries, in a form agreed with the researcher, to health and social services authorities; this seems an excellent idea, but it is not clear how often such circulation actually occurs. We might add that one research funding body has recently set up a system for the wide distribution of research summaries to administrators and practitioners. These are typically written by the researcher, but edited by the funding body.[2]

2.81 We have not yet alluded to the research report which most researchers prepare at the end of their studies – indeed, which is the one research product specified in the standard contract. It is high time that the value of such reports is questioned. Their purpose is often unclear, especially the extent to which they are intended to serve as a management tool. While traditionally seen to be useful in bringing together all

---

[1] The journal of the Social Services Research Group (SSRG), *Research, Policy and Planning* was mentioned here; we note that this includes an 'open column' in which any researcher can publicise reports of findings, with a short summary. Newsletters of researchers' organisations can also provide a useful vehicle here, for instance that of the Social Researcher Association (SRA) and The Association of Researchers in Voluntary Action and Community (ARVAC)

[2] For further information, contact the Joseph Rowntree Memorial Trust in York. A similar arrangement has been set up by NORAS, the Norwegian Research Council for Applied Social Science, Sandakerveien 99, N 0483 Oslo 4, Norway.

findings in one place, in trying to please all, in far too many cases they please no one.

2.82 Research reports should not be required unless the principal audience for the research is the customer – and this is what he or she wants. Researchers should instead produce publications appropriate to their audience – books, articles and so forth – and give copies to the customer. If additional information is wanted, this can be requested separately; a technical report on the methods employed should always be available. This recommendation represents the potential saving of a great deal of time. Writing other kinds of publications is not necessarily quicker, but writing both a report and other publications inevitably takes longer. Some researchers currently follow the suggested practice and we heard of no argument with it.

Talking about research

2.84 Face-to-face contact is increasingly being recognised as a key means by which those concerned with policy, as well as practitioners, learn about issues which concern them.[1] Conferences and workshops help to 'bring research alive'; at their best, they provide a sense of inspiration. They also provide an opportunity to assess researchers' 'feel' for the subject and to consider whether their publications merit closer attention. Some local managers noted that, having met or heard particular researchers, they were more likely to read their work subsequently.

2.84 Researchers should be encouraged to talk widely about their research findings at conferences, seminars and other forums addressed to many different audiences. While they must generally be responsive here, agreeing to give papers when asked, they can take the initiative to set up conferences or seminars on occasion. Advice and financial support from the Department(s) would be particularly welcome here.

2.85 Many comments were made about such seminars and conferences in our discussions with research users, particularly at local level. They welcomed the opportunity to ask questions of researchers, develop implications and generally talk around the issues on their minds. But there is increasing selectivity in what is attended because of time and resource constraints. Most feel that conferences are most helpful where they are informal; few seek out 'the big speech'. Practitioners prefer workshops which enable them to learn details about how to change practice. A consultant noted that he preferred to hear people talking off the record.

2.86 Those organising conferences need to be clear about the specific audience, for instance senior managers, middle management or fieldworkers, and communicate this to those who might attend; it is difficult to tell simply from a title to what level a conference is geared. It may be important to keep numbers down. Enough time throughout the day should be given for informal discussions. More cross-fertilisation between disciplines should be encouraged. Researchers should be invited not simply to give papers about completed projects but to discuss research under way. A particularly imaginative example of a regular conference for practising professionals

---

[1] See David Streatfield and Tom Wilson, *The Vital Link: Information in Social Services Departments*, University of Sheffield Social Services monographs, 1980; Marian Barnes and Tom Wilson, 'The internal dissemination and impact of in-house research in Social Services Departments', *Research, Policy and Planning*, vol 4, nos 1&2, 1986; see also Hevey *op cit*.

was called to our attention, set up by researchers for midwives. This is felt to have played a key role in raising awareness of research findings among this group.[1]

2.87 Researchers should also be open to more focussed discussions with authorities and their practitioners as well as with customers. Such development work can be very helpful to those affected and, where it is paid consultancy, can bring in useful funds. It has been argued that this is important for organisational learning: 'the importance of oral communication in a predominantly oral culture cannot be overstressed.'[2] Seminars for this purpose are discussed more fully in the following chapter (see paras 3.63 and 3.84).

Using other media

2.88 Finally, researchers should be given help and encouragement to explore new means of communicating their work. One under-exploited opportunity lies in the mass media, particularly television and radio. Most researchers with whom we spoke were deeply reluctant to go down this path, fearing distortion of their results. We have a more open-minded view. These are very powerful means of altering perspectives, used not only by the general public but by professionals working in the field. Researchers do not need to produce programmes themselves, but might be encouraged to bring good ideas to producers' attention. Of course, there are risks, but there may be ways of reducing these. A list of producers with a good track record of handling research sensitively, for instance, could be compiled.

2.89 Some research might also be usefully transmitted via both videos and audio-cassette tapes. There seems to be a fad for developing videos and we are uncertain how widely they are used. They are difficult to make well and are also expensive. But there may be areas where research findings could be well communicated by this means. Even a video of a researcher giving a talk might generate some of the enthusiasm that normally comes from hearing someone 'live'.

2.90 Cassette tapes, on the other hand, seem much easier both to make and to use. Both summaries of findings and recommendations for practice could be spelled out on tape. There are many circumstances when local practitioners could readily make use of them, for instance while driving to work. Again, some advice is likely to be needed on how to create lively and accessible information by this means. We feel it is an idea which deserves much more careful attention.

Costs of dissemination

2.91 There is no question that dissemination costs. There are the direct costs of travel or producing material, the staff costs in terms of salary and the opportunity cost, as other activities are inevitably ignored. The wider the range of dissemination efforts and the wider the range of audiences targeted, the higher these costs are because of the need to tailor products appropriately. The costs of some suggestions, such as the employment of research translators, would be substantial. From the individual

---

[1] See Ann M. Thomson and Sarah Robinson, 'Dissemination of midwifery research, how this has been facilitated in the UK', *Midwifery*, vol 1, no 1, spring 1985.
[2] Barnes and Wilson, *op cit.*, p 23.

researcher's point of view, it is also possible to do too much. One 'cost' of dissemination, rarely discussed, is that researchers can become very bored with their subject.

2.92 We cannot specify an optimal amount of dissemination. This must differ from one project to another, depending on the range and nature of the audiences for a study. Some studies warrant much less dissemination than others. The availability of researchers also needs to be taken into account. Where someone is carrying out seminal work, a heavy involvement in disseminating earlier research might seem inappropriate. On the other hand, some researchers have particular skills in dissemination and might well be encouraged to be more active in this way.

2.93 The costs of dissemination must be recognised. But they represent a very small proportion of the cost of most research. An additional week or month here and there of research time, combined with some direct costs for conferences or publications, is extremely small compared to the benefits which may ensue. Indeed, it is the present *lack* of funding for such dissemination which deserves justification. Insufficient use of research due to lack of knowledge of the findings represents a serious waste of resources. The expenditure of more money in the cause of increasing such use seems long overdue.

Getting Research in: Improving Research Use

3.1 You can lead a horse to water, we are taught, but you can't make it drink. In discussing dissemination, we have been exploring means of bringing the water closer to the horse – but there remains a need for him to put his head down and *use* what is available. In this chapter, we explore measures which may help to increase the use of research, whether directly or indirectly, in the short or longer term.

3.2 As in the preceding chapter, we begin with a short discussion of the current use of research and some problems. Again, we do not intend to imply that research is not currently used. Much of it reaches and is used expressly by the audience(s) for whom it was intended. But, again, there are some measures which can be taken to increase use.

The use of research

3.3 This project did not set out to examine systematically the extent to which research is used; such an exercise would require much more resources than we had at our disposal and a very specific brief. There are, indeed, some studies on this topic, both published and currently under way.[1] Nonetheless, we did explore informally with both customers and those in health and local authorities their own use of research and some researchers told us how their own findings had been used. Some comments are appropriate here.

3.4 It is evident that much research does get directly used – at many different levels and in many different ways. Some customers told us about studies they (or their predecessors) had commissioned and used immediately in some way. Research had helped them respond to Parliamentary Questions, fed into particular committees and reviews and in some cases had led directly to proposals for policy change, including legislation. Research had found its way into guidance documents and training materials. It had been passed down the line – to other Divisions, Regions and elsewhere – and used to provide guidance to the field, for instance with respect to planning. Less visibly, it had helped inform decisions made, for instance helping customers to confirm that they were on the right track or, indeed, to decide *not* to take a matter further.

3.5 Many customers also acknowledged that they used research indirectly, suggesting that it had affected their thinking on an issue or, in the words of one, served as 'climate creation'. Research was seen to be useful in helping to identify the right questions, to demolish misconceptions and 'to destabilise professional ways of doing things'. Research was viewed as more than the mere collection of facts and researchers'

---

[1] See, for instance, in the UK: Patricia Thomas, *The Aims and Outcomes of Social Policy Research*, London: Croom Helm, 1985; in the US: Carol Hirshon Weiss, 'Knowledge creep and decision accretion', *Knowledge: Creation, Diffusion, Utilisation*, Vol 1, No. 3, March, 1980. We are also aware that work is currently under way in this area both by Mary Henkel at Brunel University and David Smith at the Policy Studies Institute. There are undoubtedly others.

analytical approach was highly welcome; as one customer put it: 'thinking time is something you've got to buy in'.

3.6 People at local level, in local and health authorities, were also conscious of using research both directly and indirectly. Those at senior levels were most able to point to particular studies which had helped to influence policy or planning, but practitioners too could see ways in which research had influenced them. In-service training courses used research directly as part of their teaching material. Sometimes specific instrumentation had been used. As at national level, it was argued that much research was not put to direct use, but was helpful in clarifying thinking or backing up decisions already made. Research was also helpful in 'shaking us up, making us re-examine our ideas' and 'taking us out of the here and now'.

3.7 Researchers themselves were sometimes aware of the use of their findings, particularly among the academic community. Those at universities noted their own use of research in day-to-day teaching. Some stressed the importance of links between their different activities; as one psychologist told us: 'we try to make everything serve everything else: teaching, clinical work and research.' Many viewed themselves as part of a chain in the development of understanding of an issue.

3.8 Some researchers were also aware of other kinds of use of their work at local level, for instance through 'development' or consultancy work with both policy-makers and practitioners in their areas. Some instanced clear examples of the use of their data in local or health authority planning and of research findings changing practice or affecting the development of new schemes. Some were highly conscious of the use of their work because of direct inquiries: 'We know our work is used, because we get so many letters'. On the other hand, few felt they were aware of *all* such use.

3.9 Some research was also used in very practical ways. Some medical researchers, for instance, noted that close scrutiny was given to their results by the drugs industry. They were also debriefed themselves; as one put it: 'they squeeze us dry'. Similarly, those working in the field of private care found the providers a receptive audience. Research findings were also used by individual pressure groups to help support their case.

3.10 Finally, it is clear that researchers themselves get used, both at national and local level. One senior official in the DH had created his own register of research units and researchers in his field, detailing the subjects of their research and listing addresses and telephone numbers, to assist contact. When he needed advice on a pressing policy question, he called them in. Some researchers noted their involvement on official committees and working parties. Consultancy work at local level is also a means of using researchers; local managers and officers found discussions with researchers very valuable, enabling them to tease out ideas and ask questions. Some maintained contacts with local universities, research units or medical schools, using these to find out where pertinent research was going on. As one said: 'If we shout what we want, things will come out of the woodwork.'

Some problems

3.11 There is wide agreement, however, that the findings of many studies do not get adequately used – or used at all. Major decisions seem to be taken with no serious attention to research results. In some cases, this is due to insufficient dissemination, explored in the preceding chapter. But in others, the story is more complicated. Getting research used is more difficult than just letting people know it is there. Reports are received, discussions held, but nothing more is done. As one official noted, 'the paranoia of researchers that no one reads their work is somewhat founded'. In addition, researchers themselves are not always well used.

3.12 Why is research ignored? There are both political and practical causes, as well as problems arising from the nature of the research itself.

3.13 Probably the most important reason for lack of direct use of research relates to political will. It would be highly naive to expect every recommendation to be translated immediately into practice. Decisions are not framed solely on the basis of information gained through research. All Governments necessarily have their own views about the appropriate direction of policy. Furthermore, powerful interests, including professional bodies, may set up considerable resistance to change. It might be added that the funding of research itself is often a political decision, research being commissioned not to be used but to say that it was going on.

3.14 Practical barriers to research use, in contrast, relate heavily to the accessibility of research. The *quality* of presentation is crucial here. Many research reports are long and unfocussed; those for whom they are written may judge that making an effort to read them is not a good investment of valuable administrative time. One customer told us: 'If it's not easy to get into, I toss it to others and ask them to let me know what's in it'. There are also many competing pressures; research is often 'at the bottom of the pile.' The sheer lack of time for long-winded reports is a strong complaint from many quarters.

3.15 In addition, both the salience and the practicability of findings are often unclear. Recommendations are often framed with little understanding of the perspective of the person taking the issue forward and therefore lack cogency. Sometimes research demonstrates a problem with great clarity, but academic caution hinders direct advice. It is common for recommendations to be specified with insufficient precision, so that they cannot be implemented without considerable additional work.

3.16 There are also key questions of *who* reads research findings. Ideally, they should be read by officials with sufficient experience and expertise to judge their importance. Where reports are difficult to digest, however, they tend to be passed down the line, with decisions about their significance taken by junior staff. Equally significantly, such reports are less likely to be passed *up* the hierarchy to those who are most in a position to act on them. This is central to their direct use within the DH/DSS.

3.17 Another key problem is timing; a study is commissioned when an issue is heavy on a customer's agenda, but by the time the results come in, the problem has had to be confronted and is seen to be 'solved'. This is exacerbated by the fact that officials are constantly being redeployed; whereas one customer may have found an issue pressing, his successor may well have different priorities. Some customers commented that they were baffled about why a study had been commissioned in the first place. Such issues cause considerable frustration among customers and researchers alike.

3.18 It is commonly argued that government officials do not give a high priority to research. Our discussions tended to confirm this view, at least among some; they neither sought research out nor gave it much attention when it was on their desks.

To some extent, this may be due to low expectations arising from disappointment with research over time. But the systems for reversing such a cycle are themselves highly limited. Most customers seemed to have no ready means of finding out what research had been carried out on a subject and rarely attended conferences or got to know the people working in their field. Some felt this was a situation which should be changed.

3.19 It was also called to our attention that a lack of priority to research is reflected in the organisational structure of the Departments. In particular, research management is not represented at the highest policy making level. This, it is said, means that a push from the top to attend to research is missing.

3.20 These problems, it can be seen, arise from both sides. Some researchers are not skilled in making their findings useful or take no interest in trying to do so. Some customers never become engaged in the work which they sponsor, providing little direction to their researchers at the beginning or throughout the project. A number of researchers, even those working over many years for the Department, do not know who their customers are; as one said ruefully: 'I think we met one once'.

3.21 The nature of individual research projects also affects both the extent and kind of use made of them. Some studies were never intended to be useful for immediate policy needs or practical action, having been commissioned to explore a general problem with no set idea of what might come from the results. Some studies are not framed in a way to affect a pressing issue. Furthermore, in some cases, there may be little that can be done; several customers referred to this kind of work as 'so what? research', as that is the inevitable response to the information collected.

3.22 Although our exercise was expressly not concerned with the issue of quality, we cannot omit it altogether. Some customers told us of research which they felt was not worth using, having been poorly conceived, badly executed or with recommendations which did not follow from the data. In some cases, the researchers had not followed the initial specification; this was the source of some anger from the commissioning customers. On the other side, some researchers felt that they had been pressed into inappropriate projects by customers with little understanding of what is a researchable problem. Projects had been set up, they felt, whose outcome was inevitably the generation of non-useful information.

3.23 Most of these considerations apply equally at local level. Political problems, including lack of resources, mitigate against the use of many research findings. There is again a lack of time to root around for potential research results ('it's hard to get our heads above the blockade'). Some local officials argued that little research was carried out relevant to their needs, or which reflected an awareness of their problems. Again, there were inadequate links between those responsible for services and those in a direct research or research advisory capacity.

3.24 There may be particular problems in gaining responsiveness to research at local level. We were told that local organisational culture is often resistant to research, particularly where it was not carried out in the area. Some professional groups are also thought to be hostile to any research which challenges existing ways of operating. One local manager described this as an 'anti-intellectual strand, a resistence to knowledge gained anywhere but at the coalface'; one nurse noted that her profession resisted anything 'which took time away from hands-on care'. This may not be so relevant to more medically-oriented research, however.

3.25 The accessibility of research is again an issue here. While local managers said they tried to keep abreast of recent writings, many found it difficult to do so. Budget restrictions have limited involvement in professional conferences and special training schemes. Many reports are felt to be too long, dry and unreadable and it is not always clear how to make recommendations operational. There is some anger at local level at the lack of attention to these issues by researchers and funders alike.

3.26 Finally, there are considerable barriers to the full use of researchers in policy-making at both central and local level. Many researchers never have their expertise tapped in any way. In part this is simply due to custom; it is not normal practice for those concerned with policy to talk frequently – if at all – with researchers. This exacerbates a general lack of trust which derives from many factors; the two groups tend to have differing ways of approaching problems, differing time scales and often differing political perspectives. Regrettably, these differences make it difficult for people to sit down together to discuss complex issues.

3.27 Not all of these problems are amenable to simple action. There is little that can be done, for instance, to increase the direct use of research which is politically unwelcome. But there are a number of steps which can be taken to improve the usefulness and use of research.

Encouraging use by customers

3.28 It is commonly assumed – and indeed we have argued ourselves – that dissemination precedes use, as findings cannot be acted upon until they are known about. But for researchers and funders alike the question of use should be viewed as *prior* to that of dissemination; it is essential to be clear *who* might use research before it can be targeted appropriately. This proposition is fundamental to increasing research use.

The determination of research priorities

3.29 Probably the simplest way of increasing research use is to increase the funding of research which is potentially useful. Customers should think ahead about the issues confronting them and consider their research needs in this light. This means taking both a long and a short-term view. By 'useful', we mean research which is likely to illuminate an issue or provide background information as well as studies which may have a direct impact on policy or practice.

3.30 The need to give careful attention to the question of use when determining what research is to be done cannot be stressed too heavily. It is not simply that, as many argue, the wrong research is commissioned. It is also that the right research is not commissioned. If research is to be used, it must first be undertaken. RMD should view it to be their role to raise the perception of research as something which can contribute to policy-making.

3.31 The system of priority themes, set up expressly to give some rationality here, seems to have a mixed response. Some customers argue that it puts unnecessary constraints on what they can sponsor. In contrast, some feel that it does not go far enough: there is a need for a solid programme of research on one topic, from which specific *ad hoc* studies might then spring. Some customers are also frustrated at the limited resources available for research in their area.

3.32 At local level, there is considerable concern that research does not reflect local needs. In part there is no system enabling their articulation. Many managers and practitioners argued for more funds to be given to research on the delivery of services, affecting social work practice or operational issues within the National Health Service at all levels. There was seen to be a need for a better understanding of professional behaviour and the complexities of organisational change. There is a need, some suggested, for more experimentation here as well as for what one consultant called 'cheap and cheerful' research addressed to pressing issues.

3.33 We would not argue that all research ought to be directly – or even indirectly – useful. It is highly reasonable to fund research whose potential use is unclear but which may develop general insights into a problem or make a longer-term contribution to general knowledge. But to the extent that customers want to fund research for use – and this was our express brief – they need to address such issues from the outset.

3.34 We return to a discussion of what research should be for – and research priorities – in the concluding chapter (see paras 5.2 – 5.12 and 5.20 – 5.30).

The commissioning process

3.35 The issue of use needs to built in at the time a project is commissioned; getting research questions framed correctly from the start is an essential part of getting it used. A clear strategy to ensure that research is designed appropriately should emanate from research managers and permeate the wider reaches of both Departments.

3.36 Where direct use is sought, customers need to think through whether they want to change practice in an area and whether research is likely to provide useful information toward this end. They need to consider whether the projected research results will be capable of being used or, given political considerations, likely to be used. The timing of results also needs to be taken into account; if a problem must be solved in the next six months, and the research will not report for three years, then the project may not be worth undertaking. Customers should also bear in mind the considerable value of indirect use of research, however.

3.37 Turning broad policy needs into specific researchable questions should be acknowledged as a creative process. Many customers may need some assistance here; they are not generally versed in the complexities of policy research. At present, the system appears to work very unevenly; some get a lot of help from both research managers and researchers (and are very grateful for it) and others get very little. Ideally, the customer and liaison officer should work together to develop general research plans. Customers should *not* be asked to specify the research they would like, but to explore the nature of the problems on their coming agendas and the kinds of information which might help them. It is the job of researchers and research managers to turn the answers into useful research projects.

3.38 In some cases, research is an inappropriate response to a problem. This may be because the issue is not readily researchable or because sufficient information already exists. Research managers should take responsibility for discouraging the launching of such projects. This may not be easy. Some customers may be keen on an idea and it may difficult to alter plans once they are under active consideration. Researchers also will not thank them for blocking potential work. Where similar research has been undertaken, systems are needed to ensure that such information is identified (see paras 3.59 – 3.61).

3.39 We welcome the introduction of a requirement for customers to specify in writing the purpose of a study from the outset, as part of the ex-ante assessment schedule. This should force attention to the issue of use and provide the basis for subsequent customers, where there is a change, to understand what had been intended from the results.[1]

3.40 Customer involvement from the beginning is also important for the indefinable sense of engagement in a project it can bring. The study becomes not simply 'theirs' (the researchers') but 'ours' (the customers', divisions', departments'). At best, a sense of excitement and anticipation may be created, making customers genuinely eager to reach the end of the project. As a research manager outside the Department put it 'you want them sitting up and begging for the answers'. Of course, the degree of customer involvement necessarily differs across areas, depending for instance on whether the research will affect national policy or local practice.

3.41 Researchers should seek to be involved with customers as early as possible in a project. This should help them to understand why they are undertaking the work and to focus their conclusions accordingly. It will also help them to appreciate the constraints under which customers work, the assumptions which they make and their views on wider issues. This will take time, but researchers should be encouraged to give such time as part of their work and be chosen in part for their willingness to do so. It is sometimes argued that researchers need to be protected against pressure from customers which might then develop, but we do not see this is a problem. Some researchers themselves commented that they were 'big boys now' and able to cope with such demands. Indeed, a number of researchers with no (or limited) experience of meeting their customers expressed considerable regret about this situation.

3.42 One customer proposed that a 'users manual' on research should be prepared, possibly by RMD. This would explain the many stages of research, particularly the commissioning process and what could and could not be expected from research – 'how to do it, how to decide what you want, how to make sure you get what you want.' We are uncertain if this could be produced in a general enough way to be useful. It would need to be simple, putting in writing issues which might seem self-evident. It might set out, more fully than in the R&D Handbook, information on the existing research units and the kinds of issues that might be discussed with them. What another customer called 'a pocket guide to research terminology' might also be included. We note a recent pamphlet for customers on 'policy evaluation' was produced by the Treasury, together with a companion volume on evaluating research and development.[2]

---

[1] We are submitting a separate memorandum to RMD on the assessment schedules, with specific suggestions for increasing their effectiveness.

[2] HM Treasury, *Policy Evaluation: a guide for managers*, HMSO, 1988 and Cabinet Office, *Research and Development Assessment: a guide for customers and managers of R&D*, HMSO, 1989.

3.43 RMD might also run seminars on commissioning research for customers. These should explore the nature of the research process – how researchers go about their work, different research methods and so forth. They would be an excellent mechanism for encouraging discussions of such issues between customers. Other seminars on findings are discussed below (see para 3.63).

3.44 Some projects do not begin with the customer at all, but derive from a bright idea of a researcher outside the Department(s), perhaps following earlier research in the area. Here, the commissioning process eventually follows similar lines as described, but the eventual customer may feel less involvement with its execution. To ensure that such projects are useful, the refereeing process should entail explicit attention to the issues of use and dissemination. Indeed, this should be practice in any case.

Monitoring research in progress

3.45 Some customers maintain fairly close working relations with 'their' researchers, discussing questionnaires, commenting on early versions of papers and so forth. Some sit on advisory groups for projects. Others seem to have no involvement at all with research which is under way.

3.46 Just as some initial engagement is important, some on-going involvement between customers and researchers can prove enormously helpful to both. Most studies should involve at least one meeting, and long projects more, between these two groups during the course of the research. These could be formal, for instance through an advisory group, or more informal and ad hoc. Both customers and researchers should be encouraged to ask for such meetings if they feel there is a particular need.

3.47 Interim discussions can help customers to gain some idea both of the progress of research and of any early findings. They may also enable them to provide some guidance on the direction taken, although they should recognise the considerable limitations on researchers here; they should not expect to direct the course of research. Meetings may be particularly useful just before research is to be written up, so that customers can explore informally the implications of the research, consider additional analysis and suggest how information might be presented. Some argue that such a system serves as a valuable 'taster', making customers more eager for subsequent information. Liaison officers have a key role role here in keeping research on a customer's agenda.

3.48 Early written material can also be valuable. Researchers might be asked to produce a short summary of their findings before they write up their results formally, to give customers a sense of what is coming out. Such information provides a useful focus for discussions and may enable customers to begin to *use* research at an early stage. They need to appreciate, however, that the conclusions may be unclear until research is fully written up; some researchers, indeed, change their views in the course of the writing process. Any early use should be careful to indicate that findings are still tentative. Customers should take the advice of the researchers, who will have a fairly clear idea about their own certainties at this point.

On completion of research

3.49 Research is not completed until it has been written up and made available to those who commissioned it. Too often, we were told, this does not occur on time.

Some delays are short, but nonetheless annoying for those waiting for results. Some are more lengthy; researchers spend the time alloted to their study in carrying out the research and then find they have no time for writing. While it is easy to see why this occurs, it should not be condoned. Researchers should respect deadlines and research managers should place great weight on seeing that they do so, unless agreements to the contrary are made with all parties. The feasibility of the timetable should be considered right from the start, with liaison officers ensuring that customers do not ask – nor researchers promise – more than is likely to be achieved.

3.50 The nature of what researchers produce is also vital. Customers should be able to understand and make use of the findings. This appears self-evident, yet it is currently a major stumbling block for many projects. There are a range of practical suggestions here.

3.51 One key problem is the sheer *volume* of material which researchers produce. This should be kept to a minimum. A large report overwhelms the reader and tends to obscure central messages. Researchers should aim to be selective in their use of information, overcoming their natural reluctance to omit data, especially where collecting and analysing them took a lot of time. Reports do not need to cover everything found out. One researcher suggested wryly that the Department 'should measure us by our conciseness' and another 'thick documents deserve to stay unread.'

3.52 It should not take a lot of time to discover the range and import of a researcher's conclusions. One key means of helping readers is the preparation of a summary of the main findings, set out at the beginning of a report. While some researchers fear that customers will then not read the main body of their report, we believe they are more likely to do so where the key points are signposted. As one customer argued 'the summary should stand alone but draw you in.' On the other hand, customers need to recognise that understanding the conclusions of some research may take effort; they need to be willing to give some time to the enterprise.

3.53 Customers should give clear instructions to researchers about what they want from the research. The nature and contents of publications should be thought about from the beginning of a project. Such discussions might usefully focus on the kind of decisions the findings are likely to affect. Reports should then be written to reflect what is wanted, with the main conclusions pointed out at an early stage. Academic or technical considerations, such as the methods followed, should be put in an annex. While some researchers will argue with this suggestion, viewing their methods to have significance for the results, they should bear in mind the nature of the interests of the audience. There is no benefit in losing readers along the way.

3.54 One issue here is whether researchers should only present the evidence or offer recommendations. Whereas some customers actively seek advice, others commission research solely for its analysis of the facts. One customer noted that a Minister is likely to ask of unwelcome recommendations: 'you mean we've *paid* for this?' Such matters should be negotiated at the start of a project. Customers should retain an open mind here; researchers often have a close understanding of their subject, arising from the considerable time spent on it, and their recommendations may well reflect this insight. Customers are under no obligation to *follow* researchers' recommendations. Researchers, on the other hand, need to be careful in how they discuss sensitive issues; they must undertake what one called 'some delicate footwork' in some cases.

They might be invited to imply recommendations in their conclusions, spelling them out in a separate memorandum to the customer.

3.55 Researchers themselves hold differing views about whether they should seek to influence policy. Some are rather passive, arguing that it is for others to decide what use to make of their conclusions. Others are more active, soliciting the interest of anyone inside or outside the policy process who will listen – via the media, pressure groups or simply influential friends. It is clear that if researchers wish to have influence, they are likely to have to work for it. It is relatively rare for research to be used with no additional effort, as there are too many competing pressures on customers' time. Indeed, journalists may be more likely to stimulate discussion with one well-argued article, however much less firmly rooted in careful analysis.[1]

3.56 In the end, of course, it is the customer who has the principal responsibility for using research. Officials need to ensure that they give research their full attention. If a report is passed on to junior staff to read, the customer should have a clear picture of what it has to say. Decisions to take an issue forward because of research – or to ignore the results – should not be taken by people with insufficient expertise to judge them. There is also a need for careful interpretation of what Ministers will bear. A number of people outside the Department(s) argued that there is an unwillingness to take risks to support sensitive research findings, although these could be presented in such a way as to receive political support.

3.57 In addition to reading reports and other written material, customers need opportunities to discuss the implications of studies with those involved in undertaking them. A great deal can be learned where issues can be explored and questions raised. Researchers should be invited in when their research is complete and fully debriefed about their findings. While this is practice in many cases, it should become normal departmental policy.

3.58 Studies of the kinds of research which are used, and how, would provide valuable information here. These might help researchers, customers and RMD to adjust their work to be more useful. We make some recommendations on this issue in the following chapter (see paras 4.38 – 4.54).

Some general issues

3.59 The use of research is not simply about the use of particular studies commissioned by individual customers. Those working in policy branches should be encouraged to be open to a much wider range of research. There is a tendency to be highly inward looking, to assume that the only useful research is that which is directly commissioned by the Department(s).[2] In fact, there is a great deal of relevant research commissioned by independent trusts and other funding bodies. RMD should view it as its role to ensure that customers are more familiar with what is available.

3.60 Some customers told us that they would welcome help in seeking out research of relevance to their area. There are a number of ways to meet this need. Some argued

---

[1] This point is made by Patricia Thomas, *op cit*.
[2] We note that this tendency has been identified as common to many government departments. See Patricia Thomas, *op cit*.

that more staff within their division would be a help; a few commented on the restrictions imposed by loss of staff in recent years. Others saw this as a role which should be played by liaison officers. We see no reason, other than lack of time, why they should not do so. We strongly urge that liaison officers should have a 'service orientation' to their work, such that they seek to facilitate, or occasionally provide, whatever research 'service' the customer most wants. Where this includes more information on existing research, they should undertake such work directly or ensure that it is commissioned. Some undoubtedly have such an orientation now. We return to the broad role of RMD in the concluding chapter (see paras 5.31 – 5.60).

3.61 A more radical, and much more expensive, proposal here is the employment of 'research specialists' within customer divisions, able to provide an interpretive capacity with respect to research. Ideally, these should fully understand customers' needs, working as part of the same division, but should also have the skills to interpret research findings so that they can be used. They should serve as a bridge between the world of the policy user and that of the researcher, keeping abreast of developments in both areas. They might write short authoritative summaries or policy briefs, to synthesise current studies within a specific context. We understand that such posts, often called 'policy analysts', exist in varying forms elsewhere and are said to be very welcome. In one country, they were said to produce digests of research described as 'the half-hour read', highly valued by administrators.[1]

3.62 Of course, it is not necessary to have permanent staff in order to obtain literature reviews or digests of current research. These could also be commissioned on an *ad hoc* basis. We propose that this is given careful attention in each policy area. Such reviews might set out an overview of current thinking on a question or the 'state of the art' in a useable way.[2] Research managers should be able to advise whether such a summary already exists. Where these are commissioned, they should be undertaken by researchers highly familiar with the field and willing to tease out the implications of research findings for action. Such reviews are not expensive compared to the funding of new research; researchers themselves may welcome the opportunity to write them, as they can be published subsequently as a review article in an academic journal.

3.63 Research seminars are another means of helping customers to learn about new developments in their field. Many customers said they would like to be able to explore issues with others in an informal way. We understand that a system of lunch-time seminars on research was instituted recently, with varying success. Some attention should be given to how these could be made more useful to participants. For instance, it was suggested that they try to cover too much on any one occasion. They may also need to be better publicised, both formally and informally. This suggestion is complementary to the proposal that seminars be set up to help customers learn about the research process (see para 3.43).

---

[1] We are endebted to Prof Geoffrey Oldham, Director of the Science Policy Research Unit, University of Sussex, for this phrase.

[2] One example of such a review—in the nursing field—was brought to our attention at the time of writing: Jane Robinson and Ruth Elkin, *Research for Policy and Policy for Research: a review of selected DHSS-funded nurse education research 1975 – 1986*, Nursing Policy Studies Centre, University of Warwick, 1989

3.64 At the risk of recommending the obvious, there is a need in some cases for better means of keeping track of what has already been funded. A filing system providing what one manager called some 'research memory' is essential. This is particularly a problem because of the regular change in posts; incoming customers need to be able to have quick access to previous work and supporting papers. Customers' files, we assume, differ considerably here, but we heard of enough problems to see this is an issue. Keeping track of completed research is a task which would fall naturally to a research specialist. It would be eased if our recommendation for a dissemination database (see paras 4.19 – 4.37) were taken forward.

3.65 The availability of a number of services may need to be better publicised. Librarians, both at the DH/DSS and at the House of Commons, play a key role in helping customers and others learn what research has been undertaken on an issue. The existing abstracting services are also helpful both to customers and to others who receive such information (see paras 2.67 – 2.68). A Selective Dissemination of Information (SDI) service is also available, passing information on new publications to customers on request. There should be a system for copying the contents pages of relevant journals to customers. Some researchers argued that there is a need for a better retrieval and indexing system at the DH/DSS Library.

Encouraging local use

3.66 Departmental policy branches, as we have stressed, are not the only users of DH/DSS-funded research. A large and diffuse audience lies in those who run the services overseen by the DH – those in local and health authorities around the country. Their needs differ according to their role and responsibilities within their organisation. The question arises of how to facilitate *their* use of research.

Involvement in determining priorities

3.67 To help research be designed for use by those concerned with local policy and practice, they need to be brought into the determination of priorities and the research commissioning process. This broad issue was highlighted with respect to NHS research by the recent House of Lords Select Committee Report on medical research. It recommended the establishment of a separate National Health Research Authority (NHRA), to play a central role in the funding of both public health and operational research for health authorities.[1] If this proposal were to be implemented, there would be major implications for the issues under discussion here.

3.68 In the absence of any such major change, however, we have a much less radical proposal. This is to ensure that those with a local perspective are represented in the research commissioning process. Panels of local people concerned with policy and practice should be used to advise on specific subject areas. These should *not* be large cumbersome committees, with representation of all interested authorities, but should be small and focussed. For instance, there could be advisory groups for research on mental illness research or primary health care, each considering research priorities in their respective areas. The members might come from local or health authorities or

---

[1] Select Committee on Science and Technology, *Priorities in Medical Research*, House of Lords session 1987 – 88, third report, vol 1, HMSO, London, 1988.

be practitioners with specific professional or technical expertise, according to the kinds of services likely to be affected.

3.69 Such committees should not be viewed as mechanisms for designing individual research projects. These would need to be worked out in detail with research managers and researchers, in the same way as described above for central policy issues. Their point is to serve as a vehicle for bringing *local* concerns clearly onto the research agenda. There is some resemblence to Research Liaison Groups, but with much greater emphasis on eliciting the agendas of those who might eventually make some use of research results. We might add that we found a number of local people to be highly knowledgeable about research, as well as having professional expertise, and this would be an excellent way of tapping such knowledge.

Getting information to users

3.70 Once research has been undertaken, it must be targeted at the local audience. The groups likely to have an interest need to be identified and their specific information needs addressed. It may be desirable to produce more than one publication, as even among local users there are many differing perspectives. Those concerned with policy, for instance, need a greater degree of generalisation, whereas those concerned with practice need a high level of specificity.

3.71 Many recommendations for dissemination to local audiences are offered in the preceding chapter (see paras 2.72 – 2.90 passim) and do not need to be repeated here. What does need to be stressed is the importance of thinking how to make research seem *salient* to the specific audience. Does it address decisions which they face and recognise the constraints under which they operate? Is it sympathetic to their problems? Suggestions for change from such a perspective are likely to be much more acceptable. Researchers should also seek to identify examples of good practice – what people do that is right – as well as what needs to be changed.

3.72 Research also needs to seem accessible, for instance attractive to pick up and read. This cannot be stressed too highly; it can make all the difference, as one manager put it, to 'how high it is in the in-tray'. Some local practitioners told us they were more likely to believe in findings which were presented in a nice way. Reports should be short and concise. Researchers might use professional advice on the presentation of their publications, for instance on graphics.

3.73 As at national level, there is strong local support for summaries or information sheets on individual projects. In the words of one social worker, these should be 'long enough to give the flavour of the complexities, subtleties and limitations but snappy enough to give us the flavour of the findings'. Such summaries can be passed around to colleagues; those with a particular interest can then seek out the larger study. Check lists for action are also useful, setting out what *should* be done, *might* be done or *should not* be done in a particular area.

3.74 For much research, there are real translation problems to make it useful, described in the medical field as the problem of 'transferring the discovery in the laboratory to services for the sick'. Researchers often describe or analyse a problem very clearly, but do not then set out practicable solutions. One commentator argued forcefully that this was 'a waste of energy' as it was inappropriate to assume 'that people will find their own solutions.' Researchers need to think carefully about their potential role in service development. They need both to address the right problems and to think about how any findings might be used. These are issues which should be addressed from the start of a project

3.75 A few people proposed that there is a need for a new tier at local level, concerned with turning research into practical recommendations, akin to the research specialist described above for policy divisions (para 3.61). Such a person would be responsible for learning about new ideas and then talking with local colleagues about them, as well as writing useful material. Indeed, some go further to suggest that the networking of such people would prove a powerful vehicle for change, as they would pass useful ideas along to one another. This could be part of the job of a research translator, discussed in the preceding chapter (see paras 2.53 – 2.64).

3.76 Some argue there is a need for training of individual policy-makers and prac-titioners in how to use research. Their involvement in *doing* research is one important means of learning to appreciate its strengths and limitations. Some of those we spoke to valued earlier experience of research when pursuing their professional qualifications. In-service training, however, provided a more immediate opportunity to get away from the desk and reflect on practice. This can set up a greater demand for information; it also affords access to tutors who can advise on where to get it.

3.77 Many local people suggested there was a general problem of gaining information on research. This may need to be solved by better organisational arrangements within their respective authorities. Some proposed the introduction of information officers to channel research and run seminars where appropriate. Some had considerable help both from local librarians and in-house researchers. We came to suspect that many were unaware of existing help, such as the availability of the DH/DSS abstracting services on-line; those working for the NHS can gain access to this service at a particularly advantageous rate.

3.78 But we also noted a strong view that the DH should be more proactive in making research accessible to local level. It was argued that the onus should be on the research funder to ensure that researchers write up their findings in a useful way and disseminate them appropriately. It was also argued that more research should be addressed to local needs – literature reviews about practice, for instance.

3.79 Researchers might also take a more active stance in publicising their work. One health authority general manager argued that they should learn who the key 'change agents' are and send material directly to them. Because of their growing flexibility to manage resources, managers have a real interest in learning about new ideas. Researchers could ask for such information when sending out questionnaires. This might also help those researched to take a greater interest in a study and look out for its outcomes.

3.80 RMD should make explicit efforts to publicise existing research at local level. Customers, too, should seek to discuss research when meeting local people. We note that some customers wanted to do more in this respect, regretting the reduction in their contact with local areas because of increased pressures on staff time. They also commented that there are few vehicles by which research findings can be passed down the line. There is a need, within the DH in particular, to review communication mechanisms between central, regional and local levels; particular attention needs to be given to how to get to those directly involved with practice.

Making researchers more accessible

3.81 In addition to seeking to increase the use of research, there is a need to address the use of *researchers*. They represent a significant resource in terms of expertise and thinking power. Through their studies often over a number of years, they are in a good position to consider the implications of new problems as they arise. This may be particularly true for those in longstanding units, who have often amassed considerable knowledge on their subject. When faced with a new issue, one customer told us: 'what we really need is help with thinking'. Researchers are often only too happy to oblige.

3.82 How can this expertise be best tapped? What is needed is access to the right person at the right time – the ability to pick up the telephone and talk to someone who understands a problem. Better still is the chance to meet to discuss it together, often at very short notice. Customers should develop systems for meeting and talking with researchers along with other academics. Such discussions might be in one-to-one meetings or in a group; the latter, undertaken under the right conditions, can often provide more than the sum of the individual contributions.

3.83 There remains, however, the problem of trust. One answer here is more informal meetings between customers and researchers *before* a specific need arises. Such meetings need to be small, to enable those involved to get to know each other and build the confidence necessary for more constructive discussions. Early discussions about research needs provide one focus. Liaison officers can play an important role in this process.

3.84 Customers can also take a lead here. Those interested in making contact with researchers should seek to get out to conferences or to visit individual units to talk to researchers there – in one customer's words 'to sniff out the field.' This is a valuable means of getting to know individuals and developing a sense of how they might be able to help in the future. Some customers do this at present, but it is becoming increasingly difficult, with growing pressures on their time.

3.85 A more structured approach is a seminar series involving both outside researchers and customers. Although neither small nor informal, this can provide a useful forum for contact if it takes place regularly with the same people. A tea break before or after the formal discussion may enable the participants to talk informally to one another. One such seminar was run by Professor David Donnison, when Chairman of the Supplementary Benefits Commission; it proved very popular with academics and civil servants (including very senior ones) alike.

3.86 Many researchers say they would be delighted to help customers in these ways. They feel they have a lot to contribute to policy and planning and regret that their information and analytical abilities are not directly used. Many have never been asked for any information at any time. There is a common lament 'we might help, if only they would trust us'.

3.87 The same considerations apply at local level. Administrators and practitioners in health and local authorities also told us that they benefitted from regular meetings with researchers working in their area. They welcomed opportunities to discuss research with those who carried it out; in the words of one, there is a 'potency beyond paper'. Interestingly, some argued that researchers should push them into action: 'researchers should come and say this is *important*; otherwise, we tend to read things and say 'that's interesting' and not follow it up'. One manager proposed that researchers should get together, on the model of a 'trade fair', so that those interested in talking to them could visit and talk to them.

3.88 Again, we found that many researchers welcomed opportunities to work with local practitioners; they said it keeps their feet on the ground, helping them to recognise local priorities and the resource implications of their recommendations.

3.89 We suspect there is a need for the DH/DSS to clarify its position on development and consultancy work undertaken by funded researchers. While we appreciate that such work takes time away from their research and reaches only a very limited audience, but it is a very good means of increasing both the dissemination of existing research and the direct use of findings. Indeed, from the local user point of view, it is probably one of the more powerful means by which people are influenced.

Some brief comments on dissemination and use

3.90 In these two chapters, on dissemination and use respectively, we have pulled together a number of ideas for improving the use of research. It is important to state here that many of our suggestions are already practice in some quarters. Our argument is that they are not *systematically* so. It is not that the research system, taken as a whole, cannot work well but that it does not regularly do so. There is a need to learn from good practice, both within the Department(s) themselves and outside.

3.91 We would also call attention to Annex 2, in which we pull together many of our ideas in a short description of good research practice.

3.92 It is important that we reiterate here the importance of a wide view of the meaning of use. It would be a sad outcome of our study if immediate direct use of findings by customers was seen as the only beneficial outcome from a project. Such use, of course, is to be encouraged, and we have made a number of suggestions for systems to facilitate it. But we would argue that our recommendations apply equally to use of research in other ways – for information, clarification, confirmation and illumination.

3.93 Finally, we would argue that there is a need for the DH/DSS to let researchers know when their research is used. Research is a very lonely activity. Researchers can spend years working on a problem with no immediate feedback and little interest from anyone. There is great pleasure in seeing it come to fruition, for instance in a publication – even more so when this is well received. But there is probably no greater source of satisfaction for most researchers – certainly those working for government departments – than the knowledge that their findings had some meaning for someone else. They learn of this all too rarely, often by accident. It is important for systems to be established to ensure that researchers gain this knowledge.

Assessing Research Use and Dissemination

4.1 One of the central aspects of our brief was a consideration of measures for assessing the *use* of research. We were not asked to explore assessment of research in a wider sense, for example its quality or other aspects of researchers' performance, such as completing on time. We have, however, given some attention to measures of research *dissemination*, in line with the remainder of this report.

4.2 Measuring the use and dissemination of research is not a simple issue. In an interim report addressed solely to quantitative measures, we set out the strengths and limitations of some individual measures as well as key issues affecting the choice of any measurement system.[1] Here, we are concerned primarily to offer some recommendations for action. As any proposals necessarily depend on the *purpose* of the assessment exercise, we begin with a discussion of this central issue.

The purpose of assessment

4.3 From the start, we understood that the main impetus for considering the introduction of assessment measures was expectation on the then DHSS to provide some justification of its expenditure in this field.[2] Yet this is only one of several purposes which can be served by such measures. We suggest that there are three distinct reasons why the DH/DSS might wish to assess the use and dissemination of their research.

4.4 First, as noted above, such an assessment may be seen as one means of helping to determine appropriate levels of expenditure on research. This entails an effort to assess the extent to which the research, taken as a whole, is useful and/or used. The aim of the DH/DSS here would be to justify current funding levels on research or make the case for an alteration in the input of resources.

4.5 Second, such an assessment may be seen as a means of discriminating between competing candidates for research funding. This involves an effort to distinguish useful and non-useful research between different subject areas, projects, programmes or researchers, with an underlying concern to apply such information to subsequent funding decisions. The aim of the DH/DSS here would be to ensure that sensible decisions are made about resource allocation within the total budget.

---

[1] Ann Richardson and Wendy Sykes, 'Assessing the use of research by quantitative measures', Interim Report to the Research Management Division, Department of Health, Department of Social Security, unpublished, November 1988.

[2] This could be seen in the brief for the research sent to four researchers in November 1987, referring to the Cabinet Office focus on value for money exercises and the economic value stemming from research. Indeed, the project itself was initially entitled 'Assessing the value of research'. This concern was later confirmed by discussions with RMD and is visible in the booklet produced by the Cabinet Office, *Research and Development Assessment: a guide for customers and managers of R&D*, HMSO, 1989.

4.6 Finally, an assessment may be undertaken in order to improve the use of research by highlighting problem areas or barriers to such use. This entails an appraisal of the performance of those within the broad research system, including potential research users, research managers and researchers themselves, with a concern to identify steps which might be taken to increase use. The aim of the DH/DSS here would be to set up a management tool for the administration of research.

4.7 Linked with the question of *why* assessment is being undertaken is that of *whose* performance is being assessed: researchers, potential users or those employed in research management. There is also a question of the appropriate unit of analysis. In the case of researchers, this might be individual projects, researchers, research units or the overall research programme. In the case of users, it might be individual customers or practitioners (or others), departmental divisions or an aggregation of all users. In the case of research management, it might be individual liaison officers or the division as a whole.

4.8 A more fundamental issue, however, is what *action* is to be taken on the basis of the results of the assessment process. Indeed, the three designated purposes are specified in terms of potential action. We were commissioned by RMD; as it does not have a direct management function beyond its own internal boundaries, there are significant differences in the kind of action it can take compared to that open to the DH/DSS in general.

4.9 First, with respect to researchers, RMD has no direct line management responsibility for them, even where they are employed fully on DH/DSS funding. This means that assessment information pertaining to researchers cannot be used directly to affect their day-to-day terms and conditions of service nor their prospects for promotion. Information collected could be taken into account, however, when future funding decisions were being made. In other words, the decision to award a further contract might be based in part on a researcher's earlier dissemination efforts, tempered perhaps according to the budget then available.

4.10 Information on researchers' performance might be used for informal discussions with researchers, however, to explore ways of improving dissemination and use. Changes in the dissemination activities of research units over time, for instance, might prove a valuable trigger for discussions.

4.11 The position with respect to users is more complicated. In both the DH and the DSS, individuals working for policy divisions could, in principle, be assessed on their use of research and steps taken to improve this aspect of their work. RMD is not, by itself, in a position to impose such an assessment, but it could provide advice to others within the Department(s) about issues to be raised. We would argue strongly, however, against such a course. There are too many intervening factors affecting the direct use of research for such an assessment of individuals to be appropriate.

4.12 In much the same way as indicated above for researchers, information on customers' use of research might be collected and drawn on in informal discussions with them. Such discussions might cover ways of facilitating and increasing research use, including developing a better understanding of why in certain circumstances research is *not* used. RMD should not be reluctant to press customers to explain their decisions.

4.13 Users outside DH policy divisions, in local and health authorities for example, are wholly outside the scope of immediate action because of the Department's limited mandate to manage. In contrast, the DSS has more scope for management control at all levels, from Regional Management Division down to local offices. We do not recommend that any assessment systems established be used to appraise the perform-ance of *individual* users, however, for much the same reasons as specified above for customers. But again, information on research use could form the basis of discussions about means of improving use, providing advice to both policy-makers and practitioners.

4.14 The one group over which RMD has an immediate management function are those directly employed within that division. In principle, the performance of individual liaison officers in getting research disseminated and used could be assessed and viewed as an input to staff appraisal. We do not recommend such a course, however, because of the limited ability of liaison officers to control outcomes. Instead, we propose that information on the dissemination and use of the research programmes for which they are responsible should provide the focus of some discussion, in the interests of improving both activities.

4.15 Despite the genesis of our exercise, we have proceeded on the assumption that all three purposes of assessment are of interest to the DH/DSS. That is, we have assumed that information is sought to help assess the utility of the overall research programme, to help make decisions about research funding and to improve the use of research.

4.16 Ideally, what is sought are clear and unambiguous measures which capture not only the direct and indirect use of research by policy-makers and practitioners but also the dissemination patterns of individual researchers. These should provide evidence of the overall utility of the research funded, the contribution of individual researchers to this end and serve within any monitoring exercise to indicate ways of improving research use. Furthermore, they should be relevant, consistent, valid, reliable, complete and clear, easy to collect and not expensive to put into operation.[1]

4.17 This ideal, of course, cannot be achieved. There is no single measure, nor any combination of measures, which can begin to address all these needs, however sensitively designed and implemented. Indeed, we can go further still. No one of the specified aims of assessment can readily be met by any one measurement system nor, with any ease, through a combination of measures. The many requirements of quantifiable measures are, as Pollitt argues 'next to useless'. As he states: 'They describe a state of grace repeatedly envisioned in the managerial scriptures but unknown in the untidy reality of our schools, prisons or government departments.'[2] In other words, one can rarely find measures which are relevant, consistent, reliable and so forth, not to mention readily and inexpensively implemented. The criteria are easy to state but very difficult to meet.

4.18 But having specified the bad news thus baldly, we would argue that there are useful steps which can be taken. Valuable, albeit partial, information can be derived

---

[1] These attributes were discussed in our Interim Report, *op cit*.
[2] Christopher Pollitt, 'The Politics of performance assessment: lessons for higher education?' *Studies in Higher Education*, Vol. 12, No. 1, 1987, p 88.

from a range of measures and we urge that some attention be given to them. Some recommendations are set out below, together with a few comments on issues which will need to be addressed if steps are taken to implement them.

Assessing dissemination: a dissemination database

4.19 Officials within the DH/DSS, both customers and RMD, are in our judgement insuffiently aware of the extent to which the research they fund is currently disseminated. This is a worrying gap in their knowledge, with serious implications both for research use and for future research funding. In many cases, information about dissemination is not available that would enable them to identify where useful ideas might be found. As a result, they cannot demonstrate the varied nature of the products emanating from research nor justify expenditure put to this purpose. This could be rectified fairly easily by the creation of what we call a dissemination database. We urge the Departments to give serious attention to this idea. As explored more fully below, it is not so much a new idea as an extension of existing arrangements and the designation of a clearer use of existing information.

4.20 What we are proposing is a sophisticated version of a traditional publication count, with data stored on line and subjected to regular analysis. Standard information would be collected on *all* formal output produced by research units, programmes and individual researchers from DH/DSS-funded research. This would include all publications – books, journal articles (academic and those for wider consumption), reports, monographs, articles in newspapers and so forth. It would also include all other forms of dissemination – papers given at seminars, professional conferences, radio and television discussions, videos and so forth. Indeed, it could also cover involvement in training and consultancy work, including efforts to discuss research results with individual authorities or practitioners. In essence, it would collect data on any form of communication which is public and objectively verifiable.

4.21 There are three purposes to such an exercise. First, and most importantly, it would provide detailed information on all visible products of research funded, demonstrating the outputs of expenditure in this field and thereby assisting judgements about appropriate expenditure on research. The data so collected could be assessed as a whole or in selected parts, for instance by subject area or research programme. We believe it would provide valuable ammunition in any defence of current research expenditure.

4.22 Second, such a database could help to extend the use of research, by providing a source of information to inquirers, initially probably only internal, about the output from funded research. Individual customers often find it difficult to keep track of what has happened as a result of research they have sponsored. This is particularly difficult where the customer changes in the course of a study. If it were possible for customers to 'call up' information on what has been published from a study, they would be much more likely to seek out such information and then use it. In time, such a service might be extended to external inquirers.

4.23 Third, and undoubtedly most contentiously within the research community, such a database could provide the basis for an analysis of the dissemination patterns of research units, programmes or individual researchers. In other words, the information so collected could be used for appraisal purposes and taken into account when future funding decisions were being made. There are very serious problems here and we cannot recommend such analysis without much greater attention to its viability for this purpose.

4.24 There is no doubt that individual dissemination patterns vary widely and that in some cases researchers could do much more to ensure that their results are made available to those who might use them. Indeed, the preceding two chapters were directed expressly to this issue. But in setting up any means of assessing such patterns, it is essential to appreciate that quantitative measures alone cannot capture the full picture of the benefits of individual projects. Put simply, however sophisticated the information, they cannot measure the *quality* of the product(s). Thus, it would be wholly inappropriate to set up simple dissemination norms (average dissemination per project) and appraise researchers accordingly. Indeed, even taking key factors into account (such as variations between different subject areas and the budget available), such measures should not be used other than as a means of supplementing other appraisal systems.

4.25 A simple (fictional) illustration may help to emphasise this point. Research programme A, within a set budget and using a set number of researchers, may produce a large number of working papers, books, conference discussions and so forth from its work. Its research may become well known by customers, local practitioners and academics alike. Research programme B, in contrast, with the same budget and staffing, may produce only one short report to the relevant customers from its work. Its work may be little known beyond that division. Yet it is quite possible that the work of the former is mundane, repetitive and of little interest to the audiences to which it is targeted. It is also quite possible that the work of the latter is insightful, novel and directly useful. It would be wholly unreasonable to give the former a higher assessment than the latter. Quantity, in short, is no substitute for quality.

4.26 Nonetheless, we believe that if such dissemination information were to be collected, some benefit might be gained from analysing it carefully to obtain some assessment of the dissemination patterns of individual researchers and units. In conjunction with additional essential information on the quality of the work, this might be taken into account when considering the funding of further research on the grounds that past dissemination performance is a reasonable predictor of future activity. It would be important for some minimum period to be specified here, to provide sufficient lapse time to allow for inevitable publication delays. We would argue strongly against the establishment of a simple ranking system (or league table) for units or the development of dissemination standards (certain amounts judged 'excellent', 'good', 'poor' and so forth).

4.27 We might add that one bonus from such a use of a database is that it would provide an excellent incentive for researchers to disseminate more widely (although see para 4.30). Indeed, this effect could be further honed. To give one example, if dissemination through practitioner journals was felt to be desirable – and used explicitly as one means of assessment – researchers would have an incentive to target their work accordingly. This would increase the number of articles directed to this audience, and thereby potentially increase the use of research results. This argument is predicated on an assumption that the existence – and use – of the database was widely known by researchers. As we argue below, this would be essential in any case.

4.28 Information on dissemination performance could also be used as the basis for discussions with researchers; indeed, it might serve as a valuable signalling device to trigger such discussions. We would place considerable emphasis on longitudinal analysis here – looking at changes in dissemination patterns over time, perhaps both the amount of dissemination and the audiences targeted. The aim should be to encourage individual units to improve their performance each year, rather than to compete with other units in any one year. Such information might be particularly useful at the time of a Chief Scientist's Visit (see paras 4.57 – 4.58).

4.29 There are, however, a number of problems associated with the introduction of a dissemination database. First, it cannot measure research *use*; research may be well disseminated but not used or it may be poorly disseminated but well used, as key users were privy to the information. If information on either usefulness or actual use of research is the desired aim, a database simply does not meet it. Secondly, a database can in no way measure the 'value' either of individual projects or of the research programme as a whole. It can provide little indication of the intellectual robustness of the research funded nor of its contribution to existing knowledge.

4.30 Thirdly, there are real issues of strategic behaviour. If it were known to be used as a means of appraisal, a database might encourage the production of a greater number of weak publications (what has been called the 'least publishable unit'), rather than a small number of good ones. This is why we have stressed the importance of taking into account quality of publication.

4.31 Finally, some kinds of dissemination will inevitably be missed. A database must necessarily focus on *formal* measures of dissemination and cannot include private or informal communications between researchers and those who want to use their findings, even where such discussions play a central role in getting research used.

4.32 We have suggested above that this database is essentially no more than an extension of systems currently in operation. RMD collects some information on research publications at present, much of which is contained in the annual R&D Handbook. But this is incomplete and the possibilities for analysis limited and probably not cost effective. Our proposal is that fuller information be collected and that attention be given to how it can be used.

4.33 A range of operational issues will need to be addressed, such as the frequency of the collection exercise and the nature of the questionnaires used. We would propose an annual collection, perhaps at the end of the academic year or tied in with the established assessment procedures. The kind of information requested should include type of dissemination and full details of when, where, and (perhaps) to whom, in addition to the usual details of title, authorship and so forth. Useful variables for analysis might include means of identifying the project and unit, subject classification, type of research, the period of the research, number of researchers and the research budget. The main informant would probably be unit or programme directors, but project directors in the case of 'one off' projects. Information might be obtained for a number of years after the end of their contract.

4.34 Systems would need to be established for processing, analysing and using the information collected. Particular care will be necessary with the interpretation of the data. If it is used to assess researchers' output, difficult decisions will need to be taken about the weighting to be ascribed to different kinds of output. Advice will be essential in understanding the choice of journals or conferences. In addition, some measures of input (number of staff, total resources available) would need to be taken into account, as comparisons would otherwise be spurious. Outputs from projects with more than one funder might cause particular problems. We have not attempted to explore these issues very fully here, as there seems litte point until the decision to establish a database has been made.

4.35 If a database is established, it will be essential for the kind of information collected and the use to which it is likely to be put to be made fully available to all those involved in the research process. All funded researchers should be aware that it is being compiled. Similarly, customers and research managers should be aware of any action contemplated on the basis of the information collected. If norms were to be developed and used as a basis for assessing research performance – contrary to our own recommendations – these should be publicly available and subject to discussion and debate. We might add that the way in which such information is presented to researchers (and others) may have a significant impact on their response.

4.36 The development and maintenance of a dissemination database will entail considerable costs. These will fall most heavily on RMD, but there will also be costs for all those involved in supplying information. The costs of analysis, in particular, might be sizeable, depending on what is done with the information. Some current routines would, however, be eased, for instance the preparation of the annual R&D Handbook on research.

4.37 It might be added that the Economic and Social Research Council (ESRC) recently decided to undertake a similar exercise. It has commissioned Edinburgh University to establish and manage a research database, derived from regular surveys of all ESRC award holders about their output (written and oral) and information already held by the ESRC. The long term intention is to provide a publicly available database managed by the ESRC.[1]

Studies of use

4.38 To the extent that the DH/DSS are interested in the degree to which the research they fund is *used*, as opposed to disseminated, the issues are much more complex. This is mainly because of fundamental questions concerning what is meant by use, explored in the introductory chapter. To recapitulate briefly, much research is used only indirectly, in the sense that it is not translated expressly into new policy or practice. Instead, it is used to change the ways in which issues are understood and debates about policy framed over time. Research is also used in other rather diffuse ways, helping policy-makers to confirm that they are on the right track or to clarify their own ideas. Even where research is used directly, it is often extremely difficult to identify such use, primarily because users are generally unaware of the origins of their ideas. Where it is used to decide *not* to take an action forward, this is particularly difficult to pin down.

4.39 Nonetheless, if there *is* an interest in identifying the extent to which research is used, some limited strategies suggest themselves. Most obvious is some kind of survey of users, researchers or research managers in addition to case studies of individual

---

[1] For further information, contact Tim Whittaker, Head of the Information Division, ESRC. The idea of establishing such a database is discussed in Bryan Roberts, 'Evaluation, dissemination and the Social Affairs Committee, *Quarterly Journal of Social Affairs*, vol 3, no 3, 1987.

projects or programmes. We would argue that some benefit would be gained from commissioning any or all of these, providing they were carefully administered and sensitively interpreted. Two main purposes might be served.

4.40 First, they would help to create a better understanding of the nature of and constraints on research use. This would facilitate a clearer consideration of steps which might be taken to improve research use, whether by users, research managers or researchers themselves. Some kinds of survey might also monitor any efforts to improve the use of research.

4.41 A second purpose to such studies would be the collection of information on the extent to which DH/DSS-funded research is used, by whom and for what purpose. This would provide some evidence on which to evaluate expenditure by the respective Departments.

4.42 We would not recommend a survey approach for the appraisal of individual researchers, users or research managers. The information would inevitably be too partial to allow such judgements to be made. Some assurance on this matter would be necessary for those being surveyed to ensure their cooperation.

4.43 Surveys might be quantitative or qualitative – or some combination of the two. In general, a quantitative approach seeks to impose a high degree of standardisation on the collection of information, obtaining data which can be aggregated and which allow statistical analyses to be carried out. Such an approach may be most appropriate where information is sought on the *extent* of use. A qualitative approach, in contrast, is normally more flexible and non-standardised, allowing relevant issues to be explored for individual cases as appropriate. The data provide a deeper kind of understanding but, of course, conclusions based on numerical counts can rarely be drawn. A qualitatitive approach may be more appropriate where some understanding is sought of *why* research is or is not used.

4.44 We would strongly urge that any survey of use should include some qualitative methods. Used together with quantitative data, qualitative information helps to qualify, illuminate, or otherwise 'give meaning' to statistics. Used alone, a qualitative approach helps to provide detailed descriptions of processes, set a context and facilitate judgements about the importance of different factors. In this context, it could help to explore the ways in which research is used, the qualities of research which make it more or less 'useable' and the factors which inhibit or enhance the use of research. It is a good means of considering how research affects attitudes as well as how problems are defined.

4.45 There are a number of ways forward. First, the current assessment schedules used by RMD (set out in Annex 1), especially the ex-post assessment forms directed to customers, provide one means of assessing actual research use. These need to be reviewed and developed to address more specifically the subject of research use.[1] This should be part of a routine monitoring of individual units, programmes and projects and has the advantage of providing information for each funded project. The system should not be made too elaborate, however, or it will not be used.

---

[1] A separate memorandum was prepared for RMD with specific comments and recommendations on these schedules.

4.46 The information collected by such a routine exercise could form the basis for discussions among both customers and liaison officers to identify problems and suggestions for improvement. Individual projects could be discussed in the light not only of the customers' assessment forms but also of information supplied by researchers about the progress and success of their study (see para 4.63). If certain kinds of research are consistently *not* used, or certain customers or liaison officers are not getting 'their' research used, an enquiry as to why might be thought appropriate. Again, changes over time might be considered. It would be crucial to bear in mind, however, the limitations of any information collected.

4.47 Second, purpose-built surveys of other well-defined categories of users could be commissioned from time to time. Such surveys are likely to be most appropriate for areas of research in which large sums of money have been invested, such as AIDS, or where there has been a critical mass of research on a given topic with practical implications, such as research on children in care. They are most likely to be viable where they focus on specific research projects or programmes. They might target the use of research centrally by individual customers (or divisions) or might consider the use of research at local level, by local policy-makers (for instance in health authorities) or practitioners. Questions about how people gain information would be particularly crucial. Surveys could also address the issue of use of researchers, both the amount and nature of such use and the benefits arising.

4.48 Such surveys might combine both quantitative and qualitative methods. One means of doing so creatively is to undertake a two-stage approach. For example, where research has led to specific recommendations for local hospital practice, a quantitative survey might explore the extent to which such recommendations were implemented. A qualitative approach might follow, exploring why the recommendations were – or were not – put into practice in different areas. Views could also be canvassed about how to improve the use of research. This might be by individual interview or group discussions, enabling those involved to respond to one another's ideas.

4.49 Surveys of research managers to explore issues surrounding research use might also be profitable. They are in a key position between researchers and customers and should be able to shed light on research use over a number of different projects.

4.50 Surveys of researchers are more problematic, but they may have some value. Most researchers are unlikely to know about the use of their research, except incidentally through individual contacts, but they too will have views on the issue. They may be aware of the demand for their work, for instance through 'fan mail', sales of books and reports and invitations to speak. They are in a particularly good position to comment on the direct use of their services, whether in development work, consultancy or more informal discussions with customers.

4.51 Another valuable means of investigating the use of research at all levels is the case study approach. A 'case' here may comprise a particular field of research (such as nursing) or a particular research programme or project. One or more cases could be selected and the issues surrounding research use teased out. This might involve a relatively small number of individual or group interviews to develop a broad picture of the use of research in one field. More ambitiously, it might include a more sizeable study, following the use of research where lessons have been translated into practical strategies and monitoring their effect over a period of time.

51

4.52 We must note some serious questions about the reliability of any survey (or case study) information collected, especially from research users. The recall of people who process large amounts of information each week may not be very good with respect to one particular exercise; it is questionable whether they could remember if or how research was used one year (or more) earlier. Indeed, this was argued by some people with whom we discussed this exercise. Furthermore, given the turnover of customers, there are problems in relating the intended function of a research project to its actual use, as the initial customer may have moved on. In some cases, it might be relatively easy to trace that person, but this might add considerably to the cost of the exercise.

4.53 Considerable initial methodological development work would be essential on any survey of use and questionnaires would need to be properly piloted. Attention would again need to be given not only to data collection but also to establishing routines for analysis.

4.54 These recommendations are not particularly cheap. Mounting *ad hoc* surveys, whether involving a quantitative or qualitative approach or both, can prove quite expensive. The case can be made that there are higher priorities on resources than assessing the use and usefulness of research in this way. On the other hand, using the standard assessment schedules to monitor research use would require only marginal increases in data collection costs beyond the initial development stage. Some costs would be incurred, however, in data analysis and in considering action to be taken.

Other review systems

4.55 We have argued that a dissemination database cannot be used on its own to appraise researchers on their performance with respect to dissemination or the use of their research. We have also noted that surveys of research use cannot be employed to assess individual researchers or research units. The question therefore arises of whether any other means can be found to assess researchers on the extent to which their research findings or their expertise are used.

4.56 We believe that the current peer review system should be expanded to give explicit attention to these issues. At present, such review is carried out both before projects are funded and after researchers' reports have been submitted. But we understand that this process is almost wholly focussed on the quality of the research, rather than the quantity or appropriateness of the products. Indeed, we understand that it is the report, rather than other publications, on which attention at the end is primarily focussed. We see no reason why issues of dissemination (and use, where known) should not be explicitly addressed at both stages. A pro forma of questions put to those carrying out such review should include sections on the extent to which the amount and kinds of dissemination were appropriate. It should be part of RMD's explicit responsibility to make information known to referees. A dissemination database would make this task fairly simple.

4.57 Research units are additionally appraised by means of a regular visit from the Chief Scientist. Again, we understand that this is wholly concerned with the scientific quality of the work carried out. While we appreciate the need for such assessment, we believe that issues relating to the use and dissemination of research should be given a higher profile. External assessors contributing to this process should explicitly be asked to comment on these issues and subsequent discussions should take such comments into account. We would note that information from the dissemination database could be used during the Chief Scientist's visit as the focus for discussion.

4.58 It should be added that, although we did not explicitly raise the subject, a number of researchers commented on aspects of the Chief Scientist's visit in the course of our discussions with them. Some questioned the need for it at all, suggesting that the initial refereeing process should be sufficient. Some felt that it required too much preparation and detracted from ongoing research activities. Finally, some commented on the adversarial style, arguing both that this was unnecessarily difficult for those involved and that it might inappropriately affect the outcome of the exercise. What is being assessed may be more a matter of researchers' ability to cope with the adversarial process rather than their ability to marshall argument and evidence or disseminate this in useable ways.

4.59 Some methods of assessment, such as peer review, appear to be under some question at present. There is a feeling that they are too subjective and need to be balanced by some harder data. But many people in the business of research management argue that a researcher's past performance is the best predictor of future work. We suggest the need for caution in dispensing too quickly with such a view. What is important is to seek means of making such information as hard and comparable as possible.

4.60 One simple idea here is for some kind of subjective assessment by liaison officers at the end of a project. This should indicate whether it was felt that the researcher had tried hard to disseminate his or her work, difficulties experienced and any other relevant comments, such as the use made of the work, where known. This would combine a judgement of the researchers involved with a judgement of their output.

4.61 Some attention might be given to introducing systems for self-assessment, that is by researchers themselves. This could be both at the design stage and when their research is completed. In the case of the former, researchers might be asked to specify a number of objectives, including the purpose of the research, methodological plans, the ways in which the work would meet customers' and others' demands (including detailed plans for dissemination) and some more mundane goals, such as completion on time. Researchers might also be asked to specify, for each target, what an indicator of success or failure might be, discussing and refining the answers with those assessing their proposals (customers and RMD). Such objectives might be further adapted or developed during interim discussions or, in the case of units, at the time of a Chief Scientist's Visit. Discussions at the end of the project could then focus on the extent to which these objectives were met.

4.62 We would argue that such a process would help to foster a more creative relationship between researchers and customers. Researchers would be able to spell out their own aims, in conjunction with those commissioning their work. Changes in methods or direction could be discussed in the light of developments during the course of a study, but would not easily be made by researchers in the absence of such discussion. The forms and timetable for dissemination to specific groups could be built into the research design. Such a system has the additional advantage of focussing the attention of both researchers and customers on means of making the particular proposal most fully useful. It could serve as a useful management tool.

4.63 It would be useful for researchers to be asked on a routine basis to comment on the outcome of their studies, whether or not this related to an initial specification by them. Collecting such information could be part of the exercise for the dissemination database. Researchers should be given an opportunity to discuss not only what dissemination they undertook, and what use was made of their results (to their knowledge), but also what lessons could be learned from the general course of their research. Some developments may have made it difficult to meet the initial aims, for instance, or new uses found for the work. Such information could then be used for discussions with customers about the individual studies[1] (see para 4.46).

Citation analysis

4.64 It is not possible to review the many means of assessing research performance without giving some attention to citation analysis. This offers one way in which research use can be measured objectively, involving a count of the occasions on which a publication is cited by authors. The principal rationale for citation analysis as a measure of research use rests on the fact that citations provide a clear indication of *actual* use. Citation suggests that the work was useful to the person doing the citing. In addition, it is apparently objective; citation analysis does not depend on subjective reports and the data are, in principle, easily verified.

4.65 We cannot recommend a heavy investment of resources in citation analysis, however, for the simple reason that it does not measure the kind of use which we believe to be of principal interest to the DH/DSS. The use to which it refers is solely academic; it does not demonstrate use by public bodies.

4.66 Although we do not recommend such a course, if there is interest in understanding the use of research by the academic community, citation data could be sought to measure trends over time for research units or programmes or research overall. An exercise could be carried out at fairly infrequent intervals using existing databases (see below) or a wholly manual count, covering a subset of research or journals. The timescale for such information would need to be even longer than that required for a dissemination database, since academic use of published work is commonly very delayed. This itself is unlikely to prove acceptable to the DH/DSS. If a decision were nonetheless made to proceed, such data could be added to the information in the dissemination database.

4.67 A few comments on the strengths and limitations of citation analysis are appropriate here. The latter are particularly critical. Perhaps most importantly, citation analysis can only with difficulty be made to cover all kinds of publication, for instance books, reports, pamphlets or even government publications. In addition, the approach tends to be feasible in practice only for larger units of analysis (not individual researchers) as the problem of missing data affects smaller units disproportionately.[2] There are also questions about the time period over which citations should be counted; the decay rate of citation frequency has been found to vary both by research field

---

[1] The Joseph Rowntree Memorial Trust has recently implemented a system for asking such questions of researchers; for further information, contact Dr Janet Lewis, JRMT, Beverley House, Shipton Road, York YO3 6RB.

[2] see H. F. Moed *et al*, 'On the measurement of research performance: the use of bibliometric indicators', Research Policy Unit, State University of Leiden, The Netherlands, 1983.

and by the relative impact of a paper (the less cited a paper, the more rapidly it will become obsolete).[1] Allowances need to be made for the variations between subjects in citation practices.[2]

4.68 The validity of the data yielded is also a complex issue. Certain research tends to be underrepresented, for example 'seminal' research the ideas from which have been incorporated into current thinking and no longer require formal citation.[3] Those who translate or refine research findings are thought to be cited more frequently. Inappropriate weight may be given to certain authors, for instance those being heavily criticised or those cited for other purposes, including 'hat-tipping' and self-citations. Citations may additionally be sloppy or inaccurate.[4] On the other hand, it must be said that a high positive correlation between citation rates and other evaluations of research quality has been found.[5]

4.69 From a technical point of view, citation analysis is very attractive. Limited resources need to be invested in data collection, as data are available for a very wide range of publications through the Science Citation Index (SCI) and the Social Science Citation Index (SSCI). In addition, if the University Funding Council (UFC) decides to use citation analysis to assess university departments, resource savings would be possible through some collaborative effort.

4.70 There are, however, difficulties. The SCI and SSCI journal sets may not include all journals relevant to DH/DSS research. The data might thus need to be supplemented by 'manual' methods, inevitably adding to the time and cost of collection. Decisions would need to be taken on whether to differentially weight journals in order to reflect their relative prestige, their circulation or the audience to whom they are targeted. Changes over time in the journal sets covered introduce problems for longitudinal analysis. There are also a host of simple technical problems, such as inconsistencies in the use of authors' initials, misspelling of names and the tendency for citations to be listed by primary authors; the data sets also show considerable bias in favour of US and other English-language journals.[6]

Some brief comments

4.71 Current concerns with the assessment of research in general have resulted in lively discussions relating to appropriate measurement systems. Reviews of the most commonly considered indicators are provided by King[7] and Cave *et al*[8] among others. These include various bibliometric measures (publications counts, citation analysis,

---

[1] G. Folly *et al*, 'Methodological problems in ranking scientists by citation analysis', *Scientometrics*, 3, 1981.

[2] E. Garfield, 'Is citation analysis a legitimate evaluation tool?' *Scientometrics*, 1, 1979.

[3] Martin Cave, Stephen Hanney, Maurice Kogan and Gillian Trevett, *The Use of Performance Indicators in Higher Education: A Critical Analysis of Developing Practice,* London: Jessica Kingsley, Higher Education Policy Series 2, 1988.

[4] *ibid.*

[5] see Francis Narin, 'Citation analysis: bibliometric techniques in the evaluation of research programs', *Science and Public Policy*, Vol. 14, No. 2, 1987.

[6] See Jean King, 'A review of bibliometric and other science indicators and their role in research evaluation', *Journal of Information Science*, 13, 1987.

[7] *ibid.*

[8] Cave *et al, op. cit.*

co-citation analysis, co-word analysis); so-called 'esteem' measures (eg awards and prizes, prestige membership of societies, review panels, editorial boards etc, invitations to contribute to international conferences and so on); quantified peer judgements (eg reputational ranking); the counting of patents and licences (suitable for certain kinds of practical/applied research); and research income and other research 'inputs' which are taken as indicators of 'relevance' or 'success' in the market place – the ability to attract research resources.

4.72 We have not undertaken a review of all these indicators for the simple reason that they are not all suitable for this exercise. Our concern has been solely research use and dissemination; we have sought to consider how any assessment system could add to understanding here. Most of those listed above were rejected as either wholly irrelevant or of only marginal relevance to the subject at hand.[1]

4.73 A few general comments and reiterations need to be added in conclusion. First, it is important to remember that all measures carry a cost and the expected benefits should justify the costs of gathering and processing the data. We do not feel ourselves to be in a good position to make such a decision; it is up to the Departments to consider how strong is their need for information and how available the resources. Clearly, it is easier to build on existing systems, such as the new assessment exercises. On the other hand, the benefits from a much wider view are considerable. Both those commissioning research and those undertaking it would gain from a better understanding of its usefulness and use. If decisions are made to proceed, it is essential for time (and resources) to be allocated to the processes required.

4.74 Second, any assessment systems introduced should be discussed widely with those being assessed and reviewed from time to time. In particular, any quantitative measures agreed upon should be fully discussed and 'their underlying assumptions . . . articulated, debated and, where possible, tested.'[2] It is particularly crucial for those involved in the analysis, interpretation and use of the data to have a thorough appreciation of the scope and limitations of any such measures, to guard against illegitimate or overambitious use of the information.

4.75 Third, there is a need to comment on the effect of the introduction of such measures on behaviour. To the extent that any measures are devised – or thought to be devised – for the purposes of appraisal, they are likely to lead to changes in the behaviour of those being so appraised. This is commonly adjudged to be a regrettable side effect, the concern being that 'behaviour will change to conform to the letter of indicators, rather than to the spirit'.[3] This will particularly be an issue where researchers' future funding is at stake. It is not simply that they will seek to produce more publications (if that is what is being counted) but they will, in consequence, do less of something else. One commentator suggested, we suspect wisely, that they will *write* more but *think* less.

---

[1] The one possible exception here is patents, which we decided to omit from this analysis following consultation with RMD.

[2] R. Gillett, 'Serious anomalies in the UGC comparative evaluation of the research performance of psychology departments', *Bulletin of the British Psychological Society*, 40, 1987.

[3] P. M. Mullen, 'Performance indicators—is anything new?' *Hospital and Health Services Review*, July, 1985.

4.76 But strategic behaviour is not always something to be avoided. It can be seen as a positive outcome of the introduction of such measures, if behaviour is changed in a desired direction and without detriment to other aspects of a person's work. In the case of researchers, this may be more attention to dissemination as a whole or, depending on the weight given, to dissemination of particular kinds. In the case of research managers and users, too, attention to their behaviour – even if not a formal appraisal – may lead to more effort directed to these areas. This effect has been noted by Pollitt:

> *'All attempts at measurement to some degree throw up issues of fundamental objectives, which in turn trigger basic values and ideologies. Intended or otherwise, this consequence is a useful and desirable property of performance assessment.'*[1]

It would be no bad thing for researchers to give more thought to issues of both dissemination and use. If this is one effect of introducing some measures for assessing their work in this way, this might be seen to be one reason to do so.

4.77 Finally, we would like to underline the broad thinking underlying our approach to this exercise. This involves a reluctance to go too far down the road of hard indicators of research performance, coupled with a belief that some such evidence would be desirable. Our position was well stated recently by Martin Cave: 'it seems grossly inadequate and potentially unfair to assess research performance purely on the basis of subjective judgement unassisted (or unhampered) by any objective information.' On the other hand, there is a need to avoid a purely mechanistic count. Available data should 'be used with discretion to inform and supplement existing procedures, to trigger questions about performance and to shed light on what factors influence productivity.'[2]

4.78 This, in a nutshell, is the essence of our approach. Assessment measures are one means of supplementing existing information. They do not replace traditional approaches to management, but enhance them. They can help to introduce a greater degree of conscious rationality into decision making by stimulating questions and challenging assumptions. The continuing need for some subjective judgements by experienced personnel is not under question.

---

[1]   Christopher Pollitt, *op cit*, p 91.
[2]   Martin Cave, 'Measuring research output', *SRA News*, February 1989, p 14.

CHAPTER 5

Some Concluding Comments

5.1 What we have addressed is not one problem but several. What we have come up with is not several solutions but many ideas concerning ways to improve the current situation. There is no one simple way to improve the use of research or its dissemination. Nor is there one clear way to measure research performance. A number of different steps to address these issues have been noted in the preceding chapters. Here, we call attention to some broader issues.

What research is for

5.2 Underlying much of the preceding discussion are a number of interlinked questions. What is research *for*? Why do the DH/DSS commission research? What do they expect to get from the exercise and who else do they expect to benefit? The answers to these questions should help other central issues fall into place, including the determination of the research agenda and what happens to the results. Surprisingly, these issues are not often addressed.

5.3 Taking, first, the question of *whose aims* research is designed to serve, according to the annual R&D handbook prepared by the DHSS, the general aim of the Department's HPSS research is:

> '*to provide objective information for Ministers on ways of improving the efficiency and effectiveness of HPSS [the health and personal social services] and Social Security by promoting improvements in organisation, operation and administration.*'[1]

5.4 Research is thus clearly to be directed towards the immediate needs of Ministers and their senior policy advisers. But this statement can be interpreted more broadly, to include attention to the needs of those who administer the services, including service managers in the NHS, personal social services and social security. It can also be stretched to include the needs of those who are engaged in service implementation or delivery – practitioners within a wide range of professional disciplines.

5.5 This ambiguity could easily be ironed out and we would argue that it should be. Statements of the purpose of research, such as that quoted above, should be rephrased to clarify that research to help local policy and practice is explicitly within the Department(s)' remit. At present, a great deal of research is commissioned on behalf of *local* interests and this is widely welcomed. We argue below that there is a need for more; we have also proposed that the local view should be brought into the research commissioning process (see paras 3.68 – 3.69). But a prior issue is the need to establish that research beyond the immediate needs of Ministers is fully appropriate.

5.6 We would also argue for a broad approach in a different kind of way. While research is intended to meet the needs of Ministers, it is important to remember that those currently in office may not always be so. It would be extremely short-sighted to

---

[1] DHSS, *Handbook of Research and Development 1988*, HMSO, London, 1988.

commission research on topics solely of interest to the particular Government of the day. It should be part of the brief of those commissioning research to bear in mind the potential needs of future Ministers of whatever political persuasion, as part of a responsiveness to the wider democratic process.

5.7 But there is a much deeper problem. This is the fundamental question of the underlying *purpose* of DH/DSS-funded research. There is considerable ambiguity here, permeating many parts of the system. It is unclear whether research is funded in order to ensure an on-going scientific capability on broad issues within the Departments' remit or to address specific problems customers face. Put another way, is research undertaken for its wider contribution to 'enlightenment' or to help with discrete identifiable decisions (or both)? This question underlies this entire exercise; there are no easy answers.

5.8 Many customers themselves have differing views here. Some say that they commission research in order to ensure that their policies are well designed. Others argue that their aims are more diffuse. They welcome the broader understanding which they feel researchers bring to issues, the asking of new questions which generally stretch and deepen their perception of policy. Some recognise the need to let some researchers embark on a subject without knowing exactly where they will go. Some are deeply ambivalent about their role; they want to fund research for its contribution to general knowledge, but feel critical of researchers who do not make sufficient practical recommendations.

5.9 A number of researchers feel that an ambivalence on this issue is demonstrated in the way they are assessed. They are conscious of some criticism for not targeting their results outside the academic community. Yet the principal assessment system for research units – the Chief Scientist's visit – is concerned solely with the scientific quality of their work. It may be that at some visits attention is given to wider dissemination activities. It is also the case that a subsequent customer review assesses customer relevance, usefulness and so forth and that all projects require customer support, involving assessment on wider grounds. But many researchers come to feel that the main basis on which further funding will be gained is the achievement of publications in academic peer-refereed journals. With little time for dissemination in any case, other kinds of activities are inevitably given lower priority.

5.10 Many researchers themselves are concerned about the role they are expected to play. They, too, are uncertain about why they are commissioned to do some research and what products are expected at the end of the day; as one told us: 'I wonder sometimes what the Department gives us money for'. There is real concern too that customers do not know what they are getting for their money; one stated baldly: 'they haven't the faintest idea what we do'. Overall, the lack of clarity in the underlying purpose of their enterprise, coupled with a lack of involvement with customers, leads many researchers to question why they are there. Some become cynical and demoralised; others find their own reasons, including a genuine interest in their subject.

5.11 We are not arguing that research should be funded for one purpose only. There is much to be said for a varied menu of research, some clearly intended to help with specific decisions and some with a more open brief. Indeed, we address a few comments to this issue below (see paras 5.20 – 5.28). But those who commission research – and those who are so commissioned – need to clarify in their own minds what business they are in. The problem at present is the existence of differing agendas and a consequent opportunity for misunderstandings to arise.

5.12 We might add here that we suspect there is also considerable ambivalence on issue of dissemination. On the one hand, it is generally perceived to be A Good Thing, to be encouraged. On the other, to the extent that it takes resources, there may be other priorities. In a few cases it is argued that the Department(s) (especially of Social Security) should be be free *not* to publish findings on the grounds that the research was commissioned solely for internal use. But more commonly, dissemination (whether by publication or other means) seems to be viewed as more of a nuisance, increasing the already heavy pressures on policy planning.

Reflections on the use of research

5.13 The greater part of this study has been directed to issues surrounding the use of research; it seems appropriate to draw together a few thoughts in conclusion here.

5.14 First, we would stress the difficulty of recognising the use of research. People simply do not know the origins of their own ideas. This extends not solely to research customers but users at all levels and, indeed, to researchers themselves. We are all guilty, at one time or another, of ingesting a good idea – from reading, listening, talking or whatever source – and bringing it forward as our own some months later. It is in our make-up that we do not keep carefully referenced footnotes in our heads. This is well expressed by Weiss, writing about those responsible for policy:

> *'[They] have great difficulty disentangling the lessons they have learned from research from their whole configuration of knowledge. They do not catalogue research separately; they do not remember sources and citations. With the best will in the world, all they can usually say is that in the course of their work they hear about a great deal of research and they're sure it affects what they think and do.'*[1]

5.15 Second, it is exceedingly difficult to *define* exact use. As noted at the outset, it is rare for research results to be translated immediately into some new legislation or administrative arrangement. Instead, it is used as one part of the analysis of issues leading to policy or as a means of examining the effects of decisions already taken. Research helps people to reflect on their responsibilities, to feel more confident about their position or to make some incremental change in their course. Indeed, research may provide a challenge to existing ways of thinking about issues, widening options about what is possible – 'in sum . . . altering the terms of policy discussion.'[2] This role is often welcomed by those who commission it. All such activity, it cannot be stressed too heavily, represents research use.

5.16 But this is not to say that all research is so used or that it is the sole influence on policy. Indeed, as one writer argues: 'If policy were formulated on the basis of individual research projects, we would be fearful for the prudent running of the

---

[1] Carol Hirshon Weiss 'Research and policy-making: a limited partnership', in Frank Heller (ed), *The Use and Abuse of Social Science*, London, Sage, 1986, p 219.
[2] *ibid.* p 210.

61

country.'[1] There are times when research findings confront other pressures, for instance to keep to a particular political line or to minimise demands on resources. Some research, we would be naive not to note, is never intended for use – but is seen, in its commissioning, to be one response to an otherwise awkward problem. And, as we have indicated, some research proves not to be useful – whether poorly executed or presented in an inaccessible way.

5.17 Our concern here is how to make as much use as possible of funded research. This means looking for ways in which it might be useful, groups who might want to take an idea further, collections of findings which jointly add up to an argument which is difficult to ignore. It means helping customers to think out from the beginning ways in which research might help them, not assuming that they can always anticipate their research needs. It means tackling the fact that ideas need to be worked on and worried over and, in some cases, impressed upon those who may, in the end, be happy to be so pushed. There is a need to confront what one writer called 'the comfortable myth that good ideas travel on their own legs'.[2]

5.18 We note that there appears to be increasing use of management consultants to undertake work in what was formerly the territory of researchers alone. This may be expressly because of a greater willingness to tackle exactly what is specified, on time, and to produce a clear and accessible report. Their work, in short, may seem more directly useful – indeed, may in certain respects be so. It may also be due to their lesser concern with achieving a publication, reducing pressure on the customer in some cases. But some customers say they prefer researchers' willingness to broaden the subject, set a wider context or just think about an issue. The work of management consultants tends to be more derivative, not so frequently increasing the sum of knowledge or understanding, and they are also expensive. Given researchers' expressed willingness to undertake short projects of the kind undertaken by management consultants, it seems a pity not to use *them* in this way.

5.19 It might be added here that there is growing attention to this issue in many other quarters. One major research-funding body, the Joseph Rowntree Memorial Trust, has recently established procedures to assess the dissemination activities of individual researchers, set up two new posts concerned with improving dissemination and started a journal for policy-makers discussing research findings.[3] The Mental Health Foundation, another research funding organisation has recently received a grant to employ a dissemination officer, to get the research that it sponsors more widely known. The Economic and Social Research Council has also placed its growing concern with these issues on record.[4] It could be said that considering the use of research is an idea whose time has come.

---

[1] Patricia Thomas, *The Aims and Outcomes of Social Policy Research*, London: Croom Helm, 1985, p 65.

[2] Patricia Thomas, *ibid.*, p 104.

[3] The journal, first published in February 1989, is called *Search*. For further information on research dissemination, contact Dr Janet Lewis, JRMT, Beverley House, Shipton Road, York YO3 6RB.

[4] A seminar on 'The utilisation of social sciences research' was held by the ESRC in January 1989, with a strong commitment from the Chairman to give further attention to this issue.

Research priorities

5.20 In one sense, it is far beyond our remit to suggest priorities for research. Yet if there is a concern to get more *use* from research, then it cannot be emphasised too highly that research should be funded which is likely to be useful. The definition of use here, of course, should be broad enough to encompass the many different kinds of use. There are a number of issues here.

Research priority themes

5.21 One key issue is the value of the system of priority themes. In our discussions, we found two different views. On the one hand, there are those who welcome the broad strategy of creating a sustained programme of research in a few areas. They suggest that it is not difficult to make judgements about the issues likely to require attention in coming years. Having such a system helps to focus researchers' ideas. Some argue, however, that the system of priority themes has not really begun to bite. There continues to be one project here and there, arriving at different times and arising out of different academic perspectives. This provides little cross-validation and, because of the timing of the commissioning process, means that research is not able to build up a clear picture over time.

5.22 On the other side, there are those who feel the system is too heavily planned at present. They argue against the arbitrary imposition of research themes, which limit customers' ability to commission the research which they view to be important. They feel there is a need for more flexibility in the system, the opportunity to respond to issues as they arise (or are identified) and to bring in more points of view. It was suggested that some areas need more research in one year than the next. A particular subject can 'become the flavour of the month, but then the taste buds change.'

5.23 There is, of course, some truth in both positions. In principle, a system of priority themes to create a clear programme of research on pressing issues makes sense – however annoying it may be for those whose own priorities get left off the research agenda. But in practice, it is evident that a range of unrelated projects are received. It may be that the priority theme system has not been in play long enough. The system should be reviewed in a few years' time, to see how it is then working. There is also a case for some diversification; there is no one right way of addressing many issues and it is difficult in any case to get researchers to truly work together. Some flexibility to meet new issues as they arise should be assured.

Stressing the local dimension

5.24 One of the recurrent themes of this exercise was the value placed on research commissioned for *local* needs – not those of the direct customer. We have already noted that the appropriateness of such research should be clarified, so that there is no doubt that it should be commissioned (see paras 5.4 – 5.5). But there is also strong pressure from many quarters for *more* such research. In the health field, this is often termed 'health services research' but the demands extend equally to service delivery in other areas. There is concern to look at provision of services and its effects both on consumers and providers. More research to help practice is also sought. While such research may have only a very local significance – or implications for only certain kinds of areas – it may nonetheless be highly valuable.

5.25 To help to set the right priorities for such research, it is vital to have some system for ensuring a local input in the commissioning process. We have proposed the establishment of local advisory panels for this purpose (see paras 3.67 – 3.69).

5.26 Where research of this kind is carried out, it is essential that the results are communicated to those who might use them. Researchers should be urged to publish their findings in appropriate outlets and to talk widely at relevant conferences and workshops. The Departments, particularly the DH, may need to consider whether their mechanisms for communication to regional and local levels are adequate. At present, the commissioning of research may be seen as one means by which customers can get issues legitimately explored. (For a general discussion of local use, see paras 3.66 – 3.80 passim.)

Some additional comments on topics

5.27 With regard to specific topics, in addition to the strong concern for more research on *local* policy and practice, there is a related concern for more 'developmental' research – as one customer put it 'looking at the Development part of R&D'. This is important at both central and local level. There is a need to monitor and evaluate existing (and future) programmes, articulated by potential users and researchers alike. In some cases, this may mean a more experimental approach to policy – introducing changes on a trial basis and using research to learn from the experience. There is also concern to look at how research can be 'turned into a product'.

5.28 We also found considerable pressure for more studies which pull together existing research – focussed literature reviews and overviews of the 'state of the art' on a particular policy or practice. These need to be updated on a regular basis. Such work, we suspect, would prove very useful, albeit academically unexciting. There was also felt to be a need for more 'quick and dirty' studies of particular problems. We might add that some researchers indicated their willingness to undertake short studies, to serve as what one called 'a hired hand', but a lack of call on them to do so.

Setting the research agenda

5.29 An underlying question here is who sets – or should set – the research agenda. Should it stem primarily from customers or should it, in contrast, be seen as the province of researchers themselves? This is an old argument, heightened by the Rothschild report in the early 1970s and the establishment of the 'customer-contractor' principle, although it is often forgotten that this was not intended to apply to social science research.[1] The intention at that time was to give greater force to the needs of the customer and may, indeed, have done so. On the other hand, the development of research units with their own particular interests and capabilities may have created pressure in the opposite direction.

5.30 Interestingly, we did not find a clear divide between researchers and customers on this issue. Many researchers are very willing to concede that customers should set their priorities, although noting that they may need help in making these operational. Many customers welcome researchers' help in this respect. Moreover, the issue of

---

[1] Lord Rothschild, *A Framework for Government Research and Development*, London, HMSO, Cmnd. 4814, 1971.

having a clear programme of research has proponents of both points of view among both groups.

Research Management Division: roles and responsibilities

5.31 As we were commissioned by RMD, it seems appropriate to pay particular attention to those issues arising from our discussions of direct concern to this Division.[1] The key questions are the extent of its responsibility for research dissemination, the nature of the management structure and individual roles. We were not explicitly asked to address these issues, but our interest in improving the dissemination and use of research necesarily draws us into them. We therefore pull together a few thoughts for consideration here, some of which were raised in earlier chapters.

The need for a strategic approach

5.32 We understand that the Division's own view of its role with respect to dissemination is changing – or at least being made more explicit. For instance, research dissemination has now been built into the Division's contribution to the Departmental Management Account. It is in a key position with regard to research dissemination and it is right that it should play a central role in this area.

5.33 But RMD needs to address the *use* of the research which it funds. This should be viewed as a central purpose of research. By use, we mean research which provides understanding and illumination, as well as research which may influence policy or practice. The importance of research for use should be set out explicitly for wide discussion.

5.34 There is a need for an overall strategy on research use. As explored in chapter 3, the process of ensuring that research is used begins at the commissioning stage of a project. Liaison officers need to discuss the potential use of studies with customers in order to design research in ways which are likely to be helpful to them. A clearer statement of intended aims may help to clarify this further. They can also play a central role throughout the course of a study, facilitating discussions between customers and researchers and pressing researchers to write up their findings in a clear and accessible form.

5.35 In the same way, there is a need for an explicit strategy on *dissemination*, set out clearly for all those engaged in the research process. Again, this begins at the commissioning stage of a project, thinking through the audiences at which a study will be targeted and the appropriate ways of reaching them. This should be spelled out in the contract and systems devised for reviewing the issue on a regular basis. The respective roles to be played by researchers, customers and liaison officers over the period of a study should be clear. Dissemination also needs to be properly resourced. It should not be assumed that researchers can find the time for dissemination in the interstices of other work.

---

[1] At the time this report was being prepared, the respective Research Management Divisions of the two Departments had gone their separate ways. We assume that our remarks have most cogency for RMD in the DH, but many of the suggestions apply in both departments.

5.36 To suggest a strategic approach is not to argue for a simple blueprint to fit every study. On the contrary, the appropriate dissemination of individual projects is likely to differ enormously from one to another. What we propose, therefore, is not a rigid plan but a set of guidelines about appropriate procedures to be followed. As noted, this should include the specification of expected outputs in the research contract, a system for reviewing such plans at some point during a project and a process for assessing the dissemination process after the contract is completed.

The organisation of RMD

5.37 There are two organisational issues on which we cannot make recommendations, as they extend well beyond both our brief and expertise. The first is the extent to which the Division should have a fuller involvement at the most senior policy-making levels of the respective Departments. Some argue that the current organisational system limits the potential influence of research, that greater involvement would give research more legitimacy and ensure that more weight is placed on its use. We cannot comment knowledgeably here; we can only argue that the issue might be addressed.

5.38 The second question concerns the way in which RMD fits within the broader organisational structure of each Department. It can be argued that RMD is not appropriately placed within the broad organisational tree, sitting in parallel with those divisions with operational responsibility. Some contend that RMD should be abolished as a separate division and that liaison officers should be attached instead to senior customers with responsibility for policy. This, it is said, would provide customers a greater sense of involvement in research and thereby a greater commitment to it. It should in principle create closer working relationships between customers and research managers. This is, we understand, the current arrangement at the Department of the Environment. We are not able to comment sensibly on the costs and benefits of such a system, but the issue may merit some attention as a change in such working arrangements might serve to increase research use.

5.39 One means of achieving similar ends with limited organisational change, practised at the Department of Employment, is 'bedding out' liaison officers in the divisions to which they work. This means physically placing them to work alongside their individual customers, enabling closer relationships to develop between the relevant people. The liaison officers become the 'tame researchers' of the division, easily accessible for discussion and seen as 'part of the team'. Such a system requires a particular structure at divisional level and clear responsibilities for the liaison officers, so that the one can 'shadow' the other; it would not work where there is insufficient overlap or where liaison officers cover a range of disparate groups.

5.40 But we can add some comments on the *internal* organisation of RMD. One issue to which we have given some thought is whether responsibilities should be reallocated to reflect an emphasis on dissemination. It could be argued that a separate dissemination section should be established within the Division, whose staff would develop expertise in organising conferences, placing journal articles, facilitating the publication of monographs and so forth. We do not recommend such a course; the reasoning here needs to be set out in some detail.

5.41 In order for research to be commissioned as appropriately as possible, it is important for liaison officers to be attached to individual customers. This enables the people involved to establish a good working relationship and develop a sense of trust in one another. Liaison officers also need to become fairly familiar with individual fields – the nature of the issues, the kind of research which may be able to contribute to them and the range and talents of researchers available. They need to understand the ways in which research might be used and the best means of getting the information out to such users.

5.42 This kind of information comes, in effect, as a package. That is, it is all part of the expertise within any one field. It is built up over time, from extensive discussions with customers and researchers. To remove one piece of the package – dissemination – from the rest makes no sense. If a separate dissemination unit were to be established, its staff would find it difficult to acquire the detailed information pertinent to the many areas covered. At the same time, an important part of the job satisfaction of liaison officers – dealing with the end products of research – would be lost. We therefore concluded that the tasks of dissemination should be retained firmly within the aegis of individual officers.

5.43 What could be done to ease their load, however, is to establish one or more clerical or junior administrative posts with expertise in the more routine aspects of dissemination. Individual liaison officers should not have to learn the details of conference venues, publishing procedures and so forth. Much of the time-consuming work of organising research dissemination could readily be carried out by someone else, making it less expensive to undertake and releasing liaison officers' time for more difficult tasks.

5.44 It might also be questioned whether in-house liaison officers are necessary in every case. Large research units, for instance, might appoint their own officer to work directly with customers, possibly with some DH/DSS funding to pay for the post (or. if the person had wider responsibilities, that part of it used for this purpose). This would reduce the barrier between researchers and customers in these cases and would enable liaison officers to concentrate their efforts where they are most needed. It would also represent a potential saving on internal costs.

Roles and relationships

5.45 How should research managers relate to their customers? There is considerable variation in customers' attitudes to RMD – from gratitude for the time and attention given to their needs to disparagement of the inability to understand them. A few, preferring to deal directly with researchers themselves, suggested there was little need for RMD; it was seen as 'just a postbag between us and researchers'. Others felt that an intermediary role was essential, but regretted that they did not get the help they needed. Addressing such issues is central to improving the use of research.

5.46 From our discussions, we would argue that the nub of the problem here lies in the varying needs of individual customers. This is partly a matter of the abilities of the individuals involved and partly one of the demands of their particular area. Some customers need much more help in understanding research than others; some fields are much more developed in research terms than others. This suggests the need for a highly flexible approach from liaison officers to individual customers.

5.47 We believe that this flexibility would best be achieved by what we call a 'service orientation' to customers. Liaison officers should meet customers not with an agenda to determine what research will be commissioned but to ask 'what can we do for you?'. The answer may be to undertake a small literature search on a specific problem, to find a researcher who could come to discuss an issue, to explain the kinds of research that might prove helpful in that area or to commission a specific project or projects. We were struck by the willingness of customers to note their need for help – or lack of it. Some liaison officers undoubtedly already have such an approach.

5.48 Liaison officers have a great deal to offer. As they gain familiarity with a field, it should be their job to think out both possible research needs and how to match these with known resources. They should, ideally, be one step ahead of customers, anticipating their research needs. This may be either new projects or ways to disseminate or use existing research. Many customers welcome the arrival of well-thought out proposals, enabling them to do something useful without the effort of planning from scratch. This suggests that there should be minimum changes in posting of liaison officers between fields, to limit the loss of their specific knowledge and relationships.

5.49 We would also argue that liaison officers have a central role in raising the status of research within the Department(s). They should view it as their task to help customers (and others) recognise the ways in which research can assist them, to see it as an important and useful element in policy-making. Put another way, liaison officers should see themselves as 'public relations' officers for research and the wider research community within the Departments.

5.50 Research managers also need to review their roles and relationships with researchers. Like customers, researchers have mixed reactions to research management. Some are delighted with the help they have received, while others feel they have been offered little assistance relevant to their needs. Some suggest there is too little openness from liaison officers, that reasons for decisions, for instance, are not explained. Too often, liaison officers seem to become a barrier between themselves and customers.

5.51 A number of issues arise here. There is a need to clarify the extent to which liaison officers are supposed to have a management function with respect to researchers or, less heavily, mainly a monitoring one. On a very practical level, there is a need to review the involvement of liaison officers in *all* discussions between customers and researchers; we suspect there are many occasions where their presence is unnecessary. We would add that liaison officers should ensure that they feed as much information *back* to researchers as possible, for instance where their research is used. This would greatly help their sense of engagement in a live process of review and forward action.

5.52 Liaison officers play a key role in dispersing information between different groups. A recent article on the subject called attention to the importance of intersecting networks in getting research known and the value of research managers in this respect. Where liaison officers are stimulated by a seminar they attend, for instance, they are likely to transmit the findings to those responsible for policy in their area.[1] It is argued that such networks should be supported, especially where they cut across traditional intellectual and institutional boundaries.

---

[1] Jennifer Platt, 'Research dissemination: a case study', *Quarterly Journal of Social Affairs*, vol 3, no 3, 1987.

Research and research management

5.53 Underlying these issues of roles and relationships is a fundamental issue of the authority of those working for RMD – and their standing with those with whom they work. Liaison officers are neither ordinary administrators, with a clear policy brief, nor practising researchers, with the professional expertise which this brings. This puts them in a difficult position in justifying – not only to customers and researchers but perhaps also to themselves – what it is they have to offer. While, research management can be clearly defined, it tends not to command the same level of respect as the activities of either of the parties with whom they must engage. This undercuts their authority and ability to persuade.

5.54 We suspect that the status of liaison officers would be greatly enhanced if they were required to be practising researchers, part-time. This would enable them to 'keep their hand in' to their own professional interests and force them, as no other means can, to keep abreast of developments – both substantive and methodological – in their field. An encouragement to publish and give substantive papers to conferences would immediately bring enhanced prestige. It would also bring a sense of involvement in their specific professional community. This is what customers look to them for and should help them to provide the service customers need. We suspect it would give greater creative fire to their work. As a useful spin-off, some research would also get done.

5.55 There are, undoubtedly, difficulties with this suggestion; it adds to the workload of liaison officers and some of the existing officers probably have little appetite for the work. It would also be a distraction for new officers who need to learn their way around the Department. In the first instance, such an arrangement might be introduced on an experimental basis. A set proportion (which might be small) of the time of a few officers might be allocated for direct research. In the longer term, we suspect that such an arrangement might raise the attractiveness of the job to committed researchers with a strong intellectual bent. This, as may be known, is normal practice for liaison officers in the Home Office Research and Planning Unit and for some research managers in the Department of Employment.

5.56 Liaison officers should also be encouraged to learn more from one another. We understand that there is currently limited formal (and informal) communication between them. This means limited opportunity both to exchange ideas and to offer each other support with the considerable frustrations of the job. We suggest that RMD set up internal workshops, perhaps on a quarterly basis, to serve as a mechanism for exchanging ideas on research management practice. As liaison officers are all located in one place, this should not be difficult to implement. Systems should also be established to ensure that those working in related areas keep each other informed about developments.

5.57 Another means of learning is greater interaction with people doing the same job both in other departments and overseas. We note that the Home Office Research and Planning Unit has regular exchanges with certain institutions, particularly in the USA, and finds this very valuable. Sabbaticals are also arranged for its researchers, to give additional time for thinking and learning.

5.58 There may be a need for a heavier management role here. We were told that liaison officers do not discuss with each other the criteria by which they judge projects, so that it is difficult to know whether they operate even approximately a common system. Attention should be given to rectifying this, creating some common criteria and arranging discussions about them. It has also been suggested that there is a need for more training. If what we call a service orientation is considered appropriate, there may be a need to look to ways of creating it and demonstrating its implications for practice.

5.59 We are aware that some of our recommendations have substantial implications for RMD staffing and related costs. In particular, if liaison officers were to be practising researchers, many more would be needed than are currently in post. If assessment measures for research use are established as proposed in chapter 4, the costs of introducing, managing them and analysing their results are likely to fall disproportionately on RMD. It cannot be assumed that they can be borne within the existing budget.

5.60 Many of these recommendations are not new. There have been a number of considerations of these issues. An earlier report on the dissemination of research, also commissioned by the DHSS, came to many of the same conclusions. In particular, it emphasised that the Department should give greater stress to dissemination and take more initiative in this area.[1] A committee on HPSS research reporting in 1982, chaired by the then Chief Scientist, also focussed attention on many of the same problems. It expressed concern at the confusion of responsibilities, urged greater attention to dissemination and noted a need for more staff. As the committee stated: 'An effective organisation for promotion, and management, of research within the DHSS is essential.'[2] Research carried out at Brunel University during the same period elicited a similar analysis of the issues.[3]

Some wider issues

5.61 Researchers are famous for widening the boundaries of the subjects they are asked to address. We are no exception. We suggest that the following issues are not unrelated to the subject of this report.

The resources available for research

5.62 Strong representations have been made to us during the course of this exercise for the need for *more* funding for research. The DH/DSS expenditure on research, although sizeable, is a very low proportion of their entire budgets. A common argument is that they should expect to spend a set proportion of their budgets on 'research and development' (R&D), in much the same way as private industry. Coupled with such a concern is the need to obtain greater public support for this work, a recognition of the considerable benefits which are gained from better understanding of health and social issues.

---

[1] M. D. Gordon and A.J. Meadows, *The Dissemination of Findings of DHSS-Funded Research: a final report*, Primary Communications Research Centre, University of Leicester, 1981.

[2] DHSS, *The Support of Health and Personal Social Services Research*, report by the Chief Scientist's Advisory Group (Chm: Prof. A J Buller), 1982, p 30.

[3] Maurice Kogan and Mary Henkel, *Government and Research: the Rothschild experiment in a government department*, London: Heinemann Educational Books, 1983

5.63 On the other side of the coin is a very real concern that expenditure on research may be cut. The focus of our own exercise on the utility of research added fuel to such anxiety. This position is not held solely by researchers. Local administrators and practitioners, for instance, expressed considerable concern that the benefits to them from research are not fully appreciated by those who commission it. Without research, they argued, they would feel very vulnerable; in the words of one social worker: 'we would be working solely on our own myths'.

5.64 A second issue regarding resources is the lack of stability in researchers' careers arising from the heavy reliance on one-off research contracts. This has been a matter of concern for many years. The lack of a clear research career directly affects researchers' ability to disseminate their findings and therefore to get them used. This is partly a matter of lack of time, as we have shown, and problems of researchers moving on to other jobs. But it is also the case that researchers may see little point in investing in good working relationships with customers and others (and vice versa) where they do not expect to continue in post. While we would not argue that all researchers should be given tenured appointments, a strong case can be made for more posts to be established of longer duration.

5.65 We recognise that some customers, concerned about the loss of control over researchers employed by research units, suggest that the establishment of more long-term posts would exacerbate this problem. Certainly, the skills and interests of such researchers affect the kind of research which can readily be carried out. But we would argue that this should be reduced by efforts to ensure that posts are filled by suitable researchers – however 'suitable' is defined (with certain expertise, say, or with the ability to research many different topics). We would also note that in the absence of such posts, there will be a loss of such skills, as researchers move to more stable employment.

The need for diversity of funding

5.66 Another pressing issue is the need for plurality of funding. There is some fear that if DH/DSS priorities are set in one direction, there will be limited alternative means of gaining funding for research into other subjects. There are a number of different issues here.

5.67 First, there is general agreement, in which we share, that there is an important role for social and health research which is not commissioned by individual customers and whose immediate usefulness is not readily apparent. A concern with direct utility, important as this is, should not become an excuse for dispensing with all other kinds of research. Some of this research may have no immediate utility for policy at all. Some may prove to have enormous practical value in the long run.[1] Researchers should be able to have a wholly independent stance. Research for the sheer spirit of inquiry should be welcomed and supported.

5.68 There is a strong consensus that the principal – but not necessarily the *sole* – funder of such research should be the existing research councils. This was, indeed,

---

[1] This is the argument of a study carried out in the medical field in the US. See Julius H Comroe and Robert D. Dripps 'Scientific bases for the support of biomedical science', *Science*, vol 192, 9 April 1976.

the conclusion of the Rothschild inquiry into the then SSRC in 1983. The need for independent funding was argued because:

> *'so much social science research is the stuff of political debate. All such research can prove subversive because it attempts to submit . . . policies to empirical trial with the risk that the judgement may be adverse. It would be too much to expect Ministers to show enthusiasm for research designed to show that their policies were misconceived.'*[1]

We would add here that such research may not be so designed, but it may have this effect.

5.69 Second, the question has been raised as to whether research of a highly practical nature should also (or alternatively) be funded by some other source. This is mainly because the DH/DSS do not form the primary audience for such research and do not assign it as high a priority as some would consider desirable. Some suggest that local authorities, for instance, should be expected to fund research relevant to their particular needs.

5.70 There is no question that the funding of specific research projects at local level should be welcomed. But this does not mean that *all* local research needs can be met in this way. Continued central funding is essential. Individual authorities are not in a position to look at issues as generically as the DH. Futhermore, there would be an inevitable reluctance to assign funds for this purpose, especially if other authorities could be induced to do so (the classic 'free rider' problem). This would mean less research in total would be carried out. There would also be great problems of dissemination here.

5.71 An alternative suggestion is the earmarking of a set amount of DH/DSS research funds for determination at regional or local level. This might help to meet the problem, but is well outside our own remit. We have ourselves proposed that systems should be set up to bring local concerns more clearly into the research commissioning (and priority setting) process (see paras 3.68 – 3.69).

Further work in this area: some suggestions

5.72 In the course of our discussions with RMD about this exercise, we were explicitly asked to make recommendations for further work in the area. Our suggestions are, in fact, very modest here.

5.73 First, there is a need for some kind of extension to this exercise. While our proposals are derived from discussions with a range of researchers, customers and other users, our sweep was necessarily limited by the period of our brief. We feel strongly that, given their importance for all those involved in the processes of commissioning, managing and undertaking research, an opportunity to reflect on our recommendations should be given.

---

[1] quoted in Peter Brannen 'Research and social policy: political, organisational and cultural constraints' in Frank Heller (ed), *The Use and Abuse of Social Research*, London, Sage, 1986, p 162.

5.74 We propose two distinct kinds of discussion here. With respect to our suggestions for improving research use and dissemination, we propose a 'dissemination phase' to explore our ideas with those who might be stimulated by them. With respect to our suggestions for assessing research use and dissemination, in contrast, we propose a 'consultation phase' to enable those who might be affected by such proposals to comment on them. This is particularly important as these proposals have not been widely discussed. In practice, discussions might cover both kinds of issue.

5.75 Such an exercise need not entail a heavy expenditure of resources. It is a matter of setting up a number of seminars, at different locations and targeted at different groups of people. Copies of the report, or the summary of recommendations, would need to be made available. Some resources would also be necessary for researchers' time, whether our own or that of others who might be brought in for the purpose.

5.76 Second, following such discussion, we would hope that there would be interest in implementing many of our recommendations. Some of these might then be usefully monitored and evaluated. There is also a need for considerable additional work to make some ideas operational, most clearly the dissemination database.

5.77 Finally, in terms of further research on this topic, there are three specific areas which might be pursued. One or more studies of research use might be commissioned; this might be particularly useful at local level, to gain a better understanding of local information needs and ways of meeting them. This is, effectively, one kind of user survey recommended in Chapter 4. Our own exercise, itself a very limited version of such a survey, was only able to call attention to some issues.

5.78 There is also a need to 'take stock' of means of turning research results into practical outputs and action. We believe that researchers (and others) in many areas are pioneering 'development' activities and there is a need to learn from them. Some are active in preparing new kinds of publications, such as guides for local practice and training material. Some may be seeking to make videos or cassette tapes about their research. Some are creating new networks so that researchers and practitioners can learn from each other. Such arrangements play an important role in helping to make fuller use of existing knowledge. We would propose that a short project be commissioned to learn more about what is going on this area.

5.79 On a highly practical note, a survey of all funded units and programmes might be undertaken to gain information on any recent research which is thought to have practical implications which could be developed with a small input of resources. In other words, it is likely that some existing research findings could be better disseminated or developed for practice at a small cost. The ideas arising should be examined and pursued as appropriate.

A commitment to research

5.80 Probably the greatest need touched on by our inquiry is for a greater *commitment* from the Departments to the activity of research. This is not simply a question of the amount of resources allocated to this end but concerns the sense of responsibility for and involvement with the output. There is a terrible waste of resources at present, arising from the willingness to commission – but not to study and then *use* – research findings. In the course of our discussions, we were told of research results which led to clear recommendations for avoiding unnecessary deaths, improving the quality of people's lives and, indeed, saving resources through changes in existing practices of service delivery. The conclusions of much other research, while less dramatic, would also have a visible impact at many different points of the health and welfare systems.

5.81 An apparent lack of willingness to take up research results is the source of some deep concern – and not only among academics and other researchers. Comments on this issue emanated from many different quarters. To some extent, the problem is viewed as a lack of interest in – or time to absorb – new information from any source. But there also appears to be a lack of respect for the rigour with which research results are achieved, a failure to recognise that they deserve more attention than the casual journal or newspaper article. This problem tends to permeate the system, from the Departments themselves down to the local practitioner. We would argue strongly that the Departments need to take a lead here, to reverse this view and demonstrate a real commitment to the research which they fund. Our recommendations, we believe, offer some practical suggestions for working to this end.

5.82 We are not alone in this view. The Report of the House of Lords Select Committee on priorities in medical research argued in very strong terms here:

> *The Committee could not fail to be impressed, from the tone of almost all the evidence they received, by the atmosphere of despondency that reflected the low morale of those engaged in medical research.'*

This was not simply a matter, the report continues, of inadequate funding, dismal career prospects or competing demands on research time. It states:

> *The overriding cause of the collapse of morale is the impression, right or wrong, that neither the NHS nor the DHSS demonstrates any awareness of the importance of research nor is prepared to devote time, effort and resources to promote it, save only when either an immediate saving of money is in prospect or when public concern, as in the case of AIDS, forces its hand.*

> *'Either the Government considers that medical research does not matter or else it has simply failed to convey to the medical community and the public the fact that it thinks medical research does matter. Whichever interpretation is right, the Government must put this right now or it will have disastrous effects that will take years to rectify.'[1]*

5.83 The Government's recent review of the NHS, perhaps in response to this plea, does express just such a commitment:

> *The Government is firmly committed to maintaining the quality of medical education and research. It recognises the complexity and special needs of these areas.'[2]*

But we would argue that it will take more than statements of this kind to reverse the genuine doubts on the issue which are bubbling up within many parts of the research community. Major decisions about policy and practice need to seem to have some

---

[1] House of Lords Select Committee on Science and Technology, *Priorities in Medical Research*, session 1987 – 88, third report, vol 1, London: HMSO, 1988, paras 3.1 and 3.2.
[2] Department of Health, *Working with Patients*, HMSO, 1989, p 38.

derivation from research.[1] Researchers themselves need to continue to make their arguments felt. There are a growing number of individuals and organisations looking out for some response.[2]

5.84 Yet we do not wish to end on a negative note. We strongly welcome the commissioning of our own exercise as a sign of interest in the question of research use. From our discussions within the Departments, we have a found a genuine commitment among many both to the particular studies funded and to research in general. Indeed, the same could be said at all levels of the system. Nor, as can be seen from the body of this report, do we feel that lack of use can be judged solely the fault of potential users. There is a great deal that researchers themselves can do to make their research more accessible and useable.

5.85 We are, in fact, quite optimistic that changes can be made. We were struck by the willingness of those with whom we spoke to address these issues. Research users at all levels really do want to make use of research and overcome barriers that currently stand in their way. Researchers, too, are genuinely committed to undertaking applied research with a relevance to policy; they are not generally wrapped up in issues solely of academic concern. It is as if both sides feel they need some small push to move their own contribution forward. If our own exercise is helpful in this way, we could not be more pleased.

5.86 In the final analysis, a commitment to research is not something which should be begrudgingly offered. It should come from within, from an excitement about what can be learned. This requires not so much a new approach from research users or researchers as an opening up of the system. We have noted many small changes which may add up to a considerable impact on the research climate. We would like to give the last word here to one researcher who voiced many of our own concerns:

> *'Research is about illumination. If we don't succeed in that, we have failed. If a person reads something and doesn't feel any wiser, then why was it done? . . . . Research should fire the curiosity and the imagination. It should not be seen as dusty, boring, laboured, unselective documents–but live, creative and exciting to hear about . . . If people feel research illuminates their understanding and it gets into their thinking, then it is of use.'*

---

[1]   One article, for instance, chronicles the lack of attention to research in the various efforts to restructure the NHS; see David J. Hunter, 'The impact of research on restructuring the British National Health Service', *The Journal of Health Administration Education*, vol 6, no 3, 1988.

[2]   A joint campaign by ALSISS/ASRO (Association of Learned Societies in the Social Sciences and the Association of Social Research Organisations) group, for instance, called The Social Science Forum, was launched with this aim. It has produced a document, *A Programme for the Social Sciences*, to further this commitment.

References

Advisory Board for the Research Councils, *Evaluation of National Performance in Basic Research: A Review of Techniques for Evaluating National Performance in Basic Research, with Case Studies in Genetics and Solid State Physics*, London: Science Policy Studies, No 1, ABRC, 1986

Barnes, Marian and Wilson, Tom 'The internal dissemination and impact of in-house research in Social Services Departments', *Research, Policy and Planning*, vol 4, nos 1&2, 1986

Booth, Tim, *Developing Policy Research*, Aldershot: Gower, 1988

Brannen, Peter, 'Research and social policy: political, organisational and cultural constraints' in Frank Heller (ed), *The Use and Abuse of Social Research*, London, Sage, 1986

Bulmer, Martin, *Social Science and Social Policy*, London: Allen and Unwin, 1986

Bulmer, Martin (ed), *Social Science Research and Government: Comparative Essays on Britain and the United States*. Cambridge: Cambridge University Press, 1987

Cabinet Office, *Annual Review of Government Funded R&D*, London: HMSO, 1986 and 1987

Cave, Martin, Hanney, Stephen, Kogan, Maurice and Trevett, Gillian, *The Use of Performance Indicators in Higher Education: A Critical Analysis of Developing Practice,* London: Jessica Kingsley, Higher Education Policy Series 2, 1988

Chillag, 'Grey literature: an underused resource', *Research, Policy and Planning*, vol 1, no 2, 1983

Comroe, Julius H. and Dripps, Robert D., 'Scientific bases for the support of biomedical science', *Science*, vol 192, 9 April 1976

Crewe, Ivor, *Reputation Research and Reality: The Publication Records of UK Departments of Politics*, Essex Papers in Politics and Government No 44, 1987

Dartington Social Research Unit, *The Dissemination of Findings in Social Work*, report of a seminar held at Dartington Hall, 27–28 January 1983, 1983

DHSS, *The Support of Health and Personal Social Services Research*, report by the Chief Scientist's Advisory Group (Chm: Prof. A J Buller), 1982

DHSS, *Handbook of Research and Development 1988*, London: HMSO, 1988

DHSS, *Social Work Decisions in Child Care: recent research findings and their implications*, London: HMSO, 1986

Department of Health, *Working for Patients*, London: HMSO, 1989

Folly, G., Hajtman, B., Nagy, J. and Ruff, I., 'Methodological problems in ranking scientists by citation analysis', *Scientometrics*, 3, pp 135–147, 1981

Garfield, E., 'Is citation analysis a legitimate evaluation tool?' *Scientometrics*, 1, pp 359–375, 1979

Gillett, R., 'Serious anomalies in the UGC comparative evaluation of the research performance of psychology departments', *Bulletin of the British Psychological Society*, 40, pp 42–49, 1987

Gordon, M.D. and Meadows, A.J., *The Dissemination of Findings of DHSS-Funded Research: a final report*, Primary Communications Research Centre, University of Leicester, 1981

Heller, Frank (ed), *The Use and Abuse of Social Science*, London: Sage, 1986

Hevey, Denise, *Linking Research and Practice: the experience of a research liaison officer*, ESRC, 1984

HM Treasury, *Policy Evaluation: a guide for managers*, London: HMSO, 1988

HM Treasury, *Research and Development Assessment: a guide for customers and managers of R&D*, vol 1, 1989

Home Office Research and Planning Unit, *Research Programme 1988–89*, London: Home Office, 1989

House of Lords Select Committee on Science and Technology, *Priorities in Medical Research*, session 1987–88, third report, vol 1, London: HMSO, 1988

Hunter, David J. 'The impact of research on restructuring the British National Health Service', *The Journal of Health Administration Education*, vol 6, no 3, 1988

Johnes, G., 'Determinants of research output in Economics Departments in British universities', University of Lancaster, Department of Economics discussion paper, 1986

King, Jean, 'A review of bibliometric and other science indicators and their role in research evaluation', *Journal of Information Science*, 13, pp 261–276, 1987

Kogan, Maurice and Henkel, Mary, *Government and Research: the Rothschild experiment in a government department*, London: Heinemann Educational Books, 1983

Martin, B. R. and Irvine, J., 'Assessing basic research: some partial indicators of scientific progress in radio astronomy', *Research Policy*, 12, pp 145–162, 1980

McLachlan, Gordon, ed., *A Fresh Look at Policies for Health Services Research and its Relevance to Management*, Report of a NPHT Working Party, Occasional Paper 3, London: Nuffield Provincial Hospitals Trust, 1985

Moed, H. F. *et al*, 'On the measurement of research performance: the use of bibliometric indicators', Research Policy Unit, State University of Leiden, The Netherlands, 1983

Mullen, P. M., 'Performance indicators–is anything new?' *Hospital and Health Services Review*, July, pp 165–167, 1985

Narin, Francis, 'Citation analysis: bibliometric techniques in the evaluation of research programs', *Science and Public Policy*, Vol. 14, No. 2, pp 99–106, 1987

Northwest Territories Financial Management Secretariat, *Performance Management and Evaluation* (draft manual), 1983

Platt, Jennifer, 'Research dissemination: a case study', *Quarterly Journal of Social Affairs*, vol 3, no 3, 1987

Pollitt, Christopher, 'The Politics of performance assessment: lessons for higher education?' *Studies in Higher Education*, Vol. 12, No. 1, 1987

Pollitt, Christopher, 'Beyond the managerial model: the case for broadening performance assessment in government and the public services', *Financial Accountability and Management*, vol 2, no 3, autumn 1986

Richardson, Ann and Sykes, Wendy, 'Assessing the use of research by quantitative measures', Interim Report to the Research Management Division, Department of Health, Department of Social Security, unpublished, November 1988

Ritchie, Jane and Sykes, Wendy (eds), *Advanced Workshop in Applied Qualitative Research*, London: Social and Community Planning Research, 1986

Roberts, Bryan, 'Evaluation, dissemination and the Social Affairs Committee', *Quarterly Journal of Social Affairs*, vol 3, no 3, 1987

Robinson, Jane and Elkin, Ruth, Research for Policy and Policy for Research: a review of selected DHSS-funded nurse education research 1975–1986, Nursing Policy Studies Centre, University of Warwick, 1989

Rothschild, Lord, *The Organisation and Management of Government Research and Development*, London: HMSO, Cmnd. 4814, 1971

Smith, Richard, 'Research policy', series of articles in *British Medical Journal* 295 and 296, 7 November 1987 to 9 April 1988

Stapleton, Brian, 'Disseminating social services research, *Research, Policy and Planning*, vol 1, no 2, 1983

Streatfield, David and Wilson, Tom, *The Vital Link: Information in Social Services Departments*, Sheffield: University of Sheffield Social Services monographs, 1980.

Thomas, Patricia, *The Aims and Outcomes of Social Policy Research*, London: Croom Helm, 1985

Thomson, Ann M. and Robinson, Sarah, 'Dissemination of midwifery research, how this has been facilitated in the UK', *Midwifery*, vol 1, no 1, spring 1985.

University Grants Committee, 'The next research selectivity exercise: consultative paper', UGC, March 1988

Weiss, Carol Hirshon, 'Knowledge creep and decision accretion', *Knowledge: Creation, Diffusion, Utilisation*, Vol 1, No. 3, March, pp 381–404, 1980

Weiss, Carol Hirshon, *Using Social Research in Public Policy Making*, Lexington, Mass: Lexington Books, 1978

Weiss, Carol Hirshon, 'Research and policy-making: a limited partnership' in Frank Heller (ed), *The Use and Abuse of Social Science*, London: Sage, 1986

Wenger, G. Clare (ed), *The Research Relationship: Practice and Politics in Social Policy Research*, London: Allen and Unwin, 1986

Annex 1
Current Assessment Procedures*

A.1.1 RMD has just established new procedures for assessing the research which the DH/DSS funds. These entail an evaluation of research before a project begins (ex ante), mid-term and on completion (ex post). The procedures involve the completion of assessment schedules by key people in the research process.

A.1.2 *The ex ante assessment process* requires the relevant liaison officer to provide details of the instigator of the study, the priority theme to which it relates, the reasons why the customer division requested the research (if relevant), the research objectives, the timetable for the receipt of findings in order for them to be most useful, the benefits which it is hoped will accrue from the research and key points on which the project should be monitored.

A.1.3 By highlighting expectations at the outset, this information is assumed to be of value in interpreting the subsequent use of the research.

A.1.4 *A mid-term assessment* is carried out annually. Progress reports are completed both by the project director and by the liaison officer. The former summarises progress to date, indicates major departures from the original plans, confirms whether or not these changes have been agreed with the Department and lists publications and presentations made on the research in the previous year. The liaison officer's report documents whether the work is on schedule, comments on the 'science' of the study and any necessary action which has been taken, notes any specific problems which require action, endorses the customer division's continuing support for the project (if relevant) and documents the action being taken if that support has been withdrawn. Recommendations are made about whether Departmental support for the project should continue.

A.1.5 Again, this information should prove pertinent to understanding any subsequent use of the research.

A.1.6 *The ex post assessment process* is the responsibility of the liaison officer, the customer division and the project director. This process takes place in two stages: four months after a contract ends and 18 months later. It collects information both on actual dissemination and use and on other relevant issues.

A.1.7 With respect to dissemination and use, the following information is requested: indications of whether there have been or will be products of research in various categories (including written unpublished, written published and oral presentations) and, at the second atage only, details of how customer divisions used the research findings. The categories of use include:

---

*   This annex sets out the assessment procedures which had recently been set up at the time of this exercise. A memorandum proposing some changes to these procedures was submitted separately to the Departments.

—Legislative changes
—Administrative action
    —changes in policy
    —changes in advice or guidance
—Practice action
—Advice on practise
—Confirming existing policy or practice action
—Further research
—Active dissemination
—None
—Other (specified)

A.1.8 Plans to use research in any of the above ways are established at the first stage and possible benefits accruing from the research are noted at the second stage.

A.1.9 Other information requested includes: information on the punctuality of the research report, whether the research met its specified objectives, a scientific assessment of the research, customer assessment of the research, the Department's view of the research as 'useful', 'possibly useful at some stage' or 'not worthwhile' and general lessons learned from the conduct of the project (about the Department's role, the scientific content of the work and the management of the project by the researchers).

Annex 2
A (fictional) description of good research practice

A.2.1 Throughout this report, we have made numerous suggestions for researchers, research managers and users to improve the use and dissemination of research. Here, we attempt to bring these suggestions into one place, by setting out a description of a fictional project to exemplify good research practice. We must stress that this should *not* be taken as a blueprint. It is impossible to create a single system for all contingencies and many other scenarios would do equally well. But it may serve to make the picture clearer by bringing together our disparate recommendations in this way.

A.2.2 At the risk of being judged to stereotype by gender, we assume below a male customer, a female liaison officer and a group of researchers. This is simply to help to make what is already a very anonymous discussion somewhat clearer.

Pre-commissioning

A.2.3 A customer faces a new problem, on which there appears to be a need for a clearer policy stance, and is unsure what is the best way forward. He is conscious that there is growing concern about the issue at local level. He discusses this with staff in his division and concludes that there is a need for some outside advice. Research, it is thought, may shed some light on the effect of various options.

A.2.4 The relevant liaison officer is invited in for a discussion about the issue, among others. She has already anticipated this as the focus of a possible research project, through her own contacts and discussions about research needs. They explore the problem, consider when information would be needed and of what kind. The liaison officer then carries out a short inquiry into what work has already been carried out on the topic. She also talks to a few local managers who have been invited to serve in an advisory capacity on research needs. She concludes that the issue has not been adequately addressed and that further research would be helpful.

A.2.5 The liaison officer has a further discussion with the customer, suggesting how to turn the policy problem into a researchable issue and exploring the kinds of research that could be undertaken. They work out a general research brief, firmed up later by the liaison officer. She also notes the names of some researchers who have done similar work in the area. They discuss their track records for producing useable work and develop a shortlist.

The commissioning process

A.2.6 Researchers on the shortlist are invited to tender for the project. One group from an ongoing unit is successful. This group has thought carefully about the likely use to be made of the study; a short amount of time for dissemination (five researcher days) after the submission of the completed report is suggested in the proposal. Their attention to the issues of use and dissemination has been one factor in their selection.

A.2.7 The researchers already know the customer, having carried out work for him in the past. An early meeting is set up at which the customer, liaison officer and researchers establish more fully what will be done in the research. This includes a statement of aims and expected outputs.

A.2.8 A research contract is drawn up, including a clear specification of the outputs from the study. This will include in the first instance a short research report, needed by the customer, plus two articles in trade journals and one academic article. A budget for this dissemination is built into the contract, somewhat larger than initially requested as the extent of the proposed dissemination has been expanded.

A.2.9 A small advisory group is established for the project, including the customer, the liaison officer and three others with an interest in the subject, including someone with local knowledge.

The research process

A.2.10 The researchers begin to undertake the work required. At an early meeting of the advisory group, the issue of dissemination is again discussed and the initial plan retained. This helps the researchers to plan their workload. The customer makes a note of how to contact the researchers, should the need arise. He encourages them to contact him at any time that his advice would prove useful.

A.2.11 At two stages in the research, there is a need for a brief meeting between the customer and researchers. The liaison officer does not attend the first, although she receives a minute about it, but does attend the second.

A.2.12 On the first occasion, there was a need to clarify the initial specification on one important point. The researchers discuss this with the customer and the initial aims are altered slightly. A note is made where relevant for subsequent review.

A.2.13 On the second occasion, the customer, having found that the issue had become topical earlier than initially expected, asks the researchers for some early results. These are offered very tentatively and accepted on this basis. In the course of discussing the issues, the customer is helped to clarify his ideas on the subject. This enables him to raise complexities with his Minister and ensure that action is not taken prematurely.

A.2.14 Towards the end of the project, the advisory group meet to discuss how the research should be presented. The researchers produce a short summary of their expected conclusions with some supportive data for this meeting. They argue that their conclusions must remain tentative, however, until they have written up the project.

On completion of the research

A.2.15 The researchers produce, as asked, a report for the customer, with a summary of the conclusions and implications. This is quite short, focusing on the main issues, but well written and presented. It is read carefully and commented on by the customer and liaison officer. A few changes are incorporated into the final version by the researchers.

A.2.16 The customer uses the report to clarify the Department's policy on the subject; he notes that there is a need to keep a watching brief on the area. The summary is circulated by the customer to other policy divisions with an interest in the subject, with a cover note.

A.2.17 A separate technical report on research methods is prepared and commented on by the liaison officer.

A.2.18 Following a set format for all projects, the researchers are asked to prepare a brief paper on the progress of the research and any problems experienced. This is not concerned with the substance of the research but with the research process. It is used as the basis, along with the initial aims, for a discussion between the liaison officer and the customer about the outcomes of the study. A report of this discussion is filed for future reference.

A.2.19 The use of the research, communicated to the liaison officer in that discussion, is passed on to the researchers involved. Both the customer and the liaison officer commend the researchers for producing a very useful and stimulating report.

Additional dissemination and use

A.2.20 At the end of the study, the researchers produce the three articles initially specified in their dissemination budget. These are additional to the other materials described above.

A.2.21 The liaison officer suggests that this would be a good subject for a large national seminar, bringing in people with an interest from other professional perspectives. She discusses this with the customer, checks that funding is available and informs the researchers that an additional sum will be made available for this purpose. The researchers agree to plan and hold such a seminar. Some advice is available from Research Management Division.

A.2.22 Over the next year, the researchers find that they are frequently asked to speak on the subject at conferences around the country, as it has become highly topical. They contact the liaison officer and request additional funding to cover their time for this purpose. They also want to produce and distribute a revised research summary, highlighting implications for local level. Funding for these activities is agreed within a specified limit.

A.2.23 Two years later, the subject has again emerged as pressing; the Minister wants further consideration to be given to the issue. He suggests the need for some research. The customer (now changed) notes in his files that a report had been prepared, but needs updating. He is also conscious that some other research on the topic has been undertaken funded by other sources. He asks the liaison officer to commission a review of all recent research, giving particular attention to the policy issues; as the initial researchers had done a good job, he suggests the work might be done by them.

A.2.24 The liaison officer asks the researchers to undertake a short review of their own and other research in this area, funded by the Department. They agree and an overview paper is prepared for the customer. This again proves useful in clarifying Departmental thinking. As the researchers feel it is likely to be of interest in academic circles, they turn it into a review article for an academic journal.

A.2.25 A further two years later, it is found that there has been a lot of research on this issue. The Department decides to hire a research translator to pull together the results from the growing body of research for local dissemination. The translator works closely with the original research team, among others, who are consulted on their contribution in the area. Although their data are somewhat out of date by this time, much of their analysis remains valid and provides a useful focus for the discussion of the subject.

A.2.26 Each year, the researchers are asked to fill in a form about the nature of their dissemination on this and other topics. The information they provide is added to the Department's dissemination database. This proves very useful for inquirers to the Department on the subject.

Annex 3
A Note on Research Methods

A.3.1 This exercise, in principle, covered the full range of health, personal social services and social security (HPSS/SS) research funded by the then Department of Health and Social Security. But it was evident from the beginning that it would not be possible to do justice to all subject areas and that it would be inappropriate to try. We therefore asked our Advisory Group to designate six general policy areas, covering health, personal social services and social security, for our attention. They selected acute services, primary health care, nursing, mental handicap, child care and social security. The last was subsequently limited to benefits for the unemployed and income support for people living in non-private accommodation.

A.3.2 We then sought to talk to both customers and researchers working with these remits. Specific names for people to interview were discussed with RMD, but other people were subsequently added, following suggestions made in the course of the study. In total, we spoke to 18 customers and professional advisors in the policy divisions covering the areas noted above. These were mostly at Assistant Secretary or Under Secretary level. We also interviewed 44 researchers, primarily academics but a few in independent research institutes, carrying out studies in these areas. Most of these were in funded units, but we were careful also to include some who had responsibility for one-off projects. These discussions were mostly by individual interview, but we also held some group discussions, where there was interest from several researchers in one unit.

A.3.3 We had been concerned from the outset to interview a range of local research users, that is people responsible for policy and practice in local and health authorities. Following some discussions, we chose two areas and interviewed people within the respective local authority social services departments and health authorities. In response to suggestions, we also spoke to a few other health authority managers outside these areas. In total, we talked to 32 people serving in various capacities and levels within social services departments and 12 people in health authorities. The great majority of these were people with a primarily administrative function, but we spoke to some practitioners, such as social workers.

A.3.4 It was clearly important to gain the perspective of people within Research Management Division. We met the Division as a group on one occasion and also talked to 8 people individually over the course of the study. We also interviewed the chief librarian of the DHSS. Finally, to provide a still wider view, we spoke to 10 people responsible for (or with experience of) research management elsewhere. This included two other departments (the Home Office and the Department of Employment), the Economic and Social Research Council, three trusts (The Joseph Rowntree Memorial Trust, The Nuffield Foundation and The Mental Health Foundation) and one overseas research council (NORAS, in Oslo), chosen because the principal researcher was in Oslo for other work.

A.3.5 Virtually all of these discussions focussed on means of *improving* the dissemination and use of research. With customers and local users, we discussed the extent to which they had used research and ideas which would help to make such use easier. With researchers, we discussed the nature of their dissemination efforts and suggestions to make this aspect of their work easier. With research managers, we explored their views on both issues with an interest in understanding what would help them facilitate both dissemination and use. Similarly, with those outside the Department our concern was with both issues, with a particular interest in discovering new ideas to pass on.

A.3.6 Our work on *assessing* research dissemination and use, in contrast, was primarily desk research. We did not feel it would be appropriate to try to discuss this in any detail with customers, researchers or others because it is such a technical subject, although we did discuss it in passing in some interviews. We also sought out people who might be able to help here and talked with them.

A.3.7 Several opportunities to explore the issues of research use and dissemination at seminars proved particularly helpful. The principal researcher was invited to be a discussant for a session at a two-day seminar on managing interdisciplinary research organised by the Economic and Social Research Council (ESRC), involving directors of research units. That session was, in effect, a group discussion on the subject of this study. In addition, she was asked to give talks on the issues at the Civil Service College and a graduate seminar at the London School of Economics. She also participated in a seminar on the utilisation of research findings organised by the ESRC.

A.3.8 We are very conscious that there are many others we might have spoken to had time permitted. In particular, we would have liked to interview more customers and more local practitioners, particularly in the health field. The fact that we did not interview more was partly because the project itself was very short; in addition, the publication of the NHS review at the time of our fieldwork meant that some people were unable to give time to our study. Right to the end, additional names were being recommended to us. Such a wide range of interest is undoubtedly predictable for open-ended studies of this sort, but even more so as ours covered such a broad range of subjects and issues.

Printed in the United Kingdom for HMSO
Dd292975 8/90 C25 G3390 10170